Throughout this book, the pronouns he, she, him, her and so on are interchangeable and intended to be inclusive of both men and women. It is important in sport, as elsewhere, that men and women have equal status and opportunities.

Waltraud Witte

Tips for Success
Ice-skating

Meyer & Meyer Sport

Original Title: Tipps für Eis Laufen/Waltraud Witte
2. Auflage
Aachen: Meyer und Meyer, 2002
Translated by Heather Ross

British Library Cataloguing in Publication Data
A catalogue record for this book is available from the British Library

Witte, Waltraud:
Tips for Success – Ice-skating/Waltraud Witte
Oxford: Meyer & Meyer Sport (UK) Ltd., 2003
ISBN 1-84126-090-8

© 2003 by Meyer & Meyer Sport (UK) Ltd.
Aachen, Adelaide, Auckland, Budapest, Graz, Johannesburg,
Miami, Olten (CH), Oxford, Singapore, Toronto
Member of the World
Sports Publishers' Association
www.w-s-p-a.org

Printed and bound by Vimperk AG
ISBN 1-84126-090-8
E-Mail: verlag@m-m-sports.com
www.m-m-sports.com

Contents

5

8

INTRODUCTION

Very little has been written until now on the subject of ice-skating and there is actually nothing about ice-skating for the general public. This book is intended to fill the gap. It is written for amateur skaters and all those who like to exercise in the open air in winter. The basic ice-skating techniques are presented in an interesting way, enabling you to learn or improve them by yourself.

Of course, this book cannot replace an ice-skating teacher or club training. However, it can help to create a foundation that can be built on later, if you are considering specialising in figure skating, ice dancing, speed skating or ice hockey. There is particular emphasis on games and exercises, skating with a partner and the use of small apparatus.

All the techniques described in this book also apply to in-line skating, and can be learned in the same way as on ice-skates.

The chapters of this book are roughly divided according to age group into ice-skating for small children, for children and teenagers and for adults and the elderly.

Small children are introduced to ice-skating in a playful way, they need visual images. Older children and teenagers want to try tricks and jumps, to skate as fast as possible or fight over the puck when playing ice hockey. Adults and the elderly are always wary of such rough and tumble activities. They prefer to practise individual steps that they can then perform to music.

If you want to learn with this book, go step by step. Just look for one technique that you want to use. Carry out the exercises presented with an eye on safety first of all, taking the technical tips into consideration. Reduce friction with the surface as much as possible, for example, you can practise in socks on a stone floor.

It is also an advantage if you can go skating with friends and family instead of alone. For one thing it is more fun to skate in company, for another, you will have a partner with whom to practise exercises.

In the pages that follow, the word 'he' is used for the sake of simplicity. This naturally applies to both sexes.

1 WHAT YOU SHOULD KNOW ABOUT ICE-SKATING BEFORE YOU START

Ice-skating is, along with skiing, one of the oldest sports in the world. There is historical evidence for both going back around 6000 years! Of course, today's equipment did not exist then. Animal bones were split and tied onto the feet. The purpose was to move about faster and more easily on frozen lakes, etc.

Later on, the present-day Netherlands became a skating stronghold. Countless paintings by famous artists, including BREUGHEL, show how popular ice-skating was in that country. In the 18th century, this enthusiasm crossed the border into Germany, as witnessed by the works of many poets. Even GOETHE wrote about his ice-skating experiences.

In the mid-19th century, the first *all-metal skate* came from America. It was attached to the shoes by two clamps, and later by screws. This gave it greater stability and made racing possible. Around the same time, the *tube skate* was invented in Norway and was forerunner of the speed ice-skate.

Figure 1: Ice-skating in the 19th Century

Meanwhile, in Canada, a skate with much shorter, curved runners appeared, which made quick turns possible: *the ice hockey skate* was born.

Up until the Second World War, ice-skating was the most popular of all winter sports. It was then overtaken clearly by skiing.

1.1 Ice-skating Today – Still a Modern Sport

Ice-skating is possibly undergoing a renaissance at the moment, as sports based on keeping your balance are fashionable at the moment. Children and young people have developed a good sense of balance due to the summer sport of in-line skating.

They therefore gain confidence more quickly on skates and are soon able to enjoy many successful experiences. The sensation of speed and almost weightless feeling of gliding are additional attractions. They are positive influences and experiences that anyone would naturally want to repeat.

Ice-skating is one of the few sports that can be carried out in the open air in winter. In flat areas it is a particulary good alternative to skiing. It is cheaper, it can be done at home, there are no long journeys and hour-long jams to cope with and it can also be done spontaneously without much preparation. During long periods of frost, frozen ponds, lakes or canals can also be skated on. The latter are especially suited for speed skating and for long "ice-hikes".

As mentioned earlier, GOETHE was also an enthusiastic ice-skater. He appreciated the sport above all for the "free, blissful feeling of liberation from the ties of gravity!" We can still have this feeling today: while skating we feel a sense of freedom and lightness, we "float", transported by lively music over the ice. A ten-year-old sums it up in these words, "Ice-skating is like flying! You feel the wind on your skin, it blows your hair in your face – it's cool!"

Ice-skating requires a well-developed sense of balance, but unlike gymnastics, for example, even in the most difficult exercises, you always keep the upright position: feet down, head up. As good balance is also important in all other sports, e.g. for all team games (football, basketball...), for racket sports (tennis, table tennis...), for snowboarding, skiing,... your progress on the ice will also have a positive effect on your performance in other sports!

A few years ago, ice-skating found its summer counterpart in in-line skating. The equipment and therefore the movements are very similar. You can carry out the following techniques described on in-line skates, even the dance steps or the two-footed spin! We could say that ice-skating has become an all year-round sport!

1.2 Ice-skating – A Sport for all Ages and Tastes!

Ice-skating is an ageless sport, i.e. anyone can do it: as soon as a small child can walk and run, he can also try this on the ice. As an adult too you can take it up and practise it for as long as your legs will let you.

Ice-skating offers movements for all sporting types: if you like to move elegantly and would like to perform small tricks, *figure-skating* is for you. If you have a sense of rhythm and like to move in time to lively music, you should learn some dance steps, and then perhaps attempt simple dances with a partner: *ice-dancing* is your sport. *Speed-skating* is dynamic and athletic, also performed in its new version called *short-track*. The energetic sport of *ice hockey* is more rough-and-tumble. And you can practise all these during the summer on in-line skates!

1.3 You're Never too Old to Ice-skate!

As with all other sporting techniques, to reach a high performance level, it is better to start young. If you just want to skate for fun, with no great ambitions, you can still learn this sport to a satisfactory level, even as an adult. Sporting experience, especially of sports which require posture and balance (gymnastics, in-line skating, ...) is a particularly good pre-requisite, but not a mandatory.

The elderly with no sporting experience should take lessons from an experienced ice-skating teacher as well as reading this book. They lack the basic experience of movement, so that an adult cannot really learn without specialist instruction.

Ice-skating is an ideal lifetime sport especially for the elderly: the gentle, gliding movement – (ice-skating should be called "ice-gliding"!) – protects the joints. As the whole body is being used, important function stimuli are exerted on the movement apparatus, the respiratory organs as well as the heart and circulatory system.

Nevertheless, you do not need to be particularly fit, as you can control the strength, speed, endurance and mobility requirements individually, and even improve them with regular practice. The most important coordinative abilities are a sense of balance and rhythm, and ice-skating will enable you to improve or at least maintain your level in both.

Ice-skating keeps you young! As HOLLMANN said, "sporting activity is the only scientifically proven way of keeping your body younger than the age on your birth certificate." In ice-skating, this phenomenon can only be reinforced by its positive effect on your mental health.

Because ice-skating makes high demands on the sense of balance, many adults are afraid – afraid of falling and making a fool of themselves. These fears have a paralysing effect. You tense up and your learning capability is diminished, the development of a feeling for the ice and the correct movements are blocked. So relax and skate with confidence!

Be proud of still wanting to learn something new in your old age. Even as an adult you are allowed to show weaknesses, nobody's perfect!

Figure 2: A senior skater getting into his stride around the curve

To get used to the equipment and the challenge to your sense of balance, you can practise exercises at home in advance, and even without skates at first, then with the equipment protected with a skate guard.

Figure 3: The ideal ice-skating outfit

2 ICE-SKATING EQUIPMENT

2.1 Clothing – What Should I Wear?

Amateur skating does not seem to have been discovered by the sports goods industry yet. There is still no particular skating "uniform" nor fashion rule. You can dress as you wish.

Wear suitable sports clothing that allows you freedom of movement and protects you from the wind and the cold. The most suitable outfit is a tracksuit or normal long trousers, pullover and a wind-resistant jacket. Do not choose trousers with legs that are too wide; catch the tip of your skates in them!

It is better to wear several thin layers rather than just one thick pullover. This allows you to remove layers progressively as you start to get warmer. If it is really frosty, you should wear a ski suit or similar, with suitable, warm underwear.

You only need one pair of socks. If you put one pair on top of another, they will wrinkle and cause painful blisters. Knee-high socks are appropriate for amateur skaters, as they also keep the lower legs warm.

You should always wear gloves as a protection against the cold as well as against injuries. At temperatures below zero, you should also protect your head with a headband or a cap. Beginners, and children in particular, should always wear at least a cap in case they fall or hurt themselves. Better still is a helmet (an in-line skating, ice-hockey or even a bicycle helmet). Knee and elbow protectors (from volleyball or in-line skating) can also be useful.

2.2 Skates – Can I Still Use Grandma's Skates?

The sports goods industry has discovered this market! In the last couple of decades, there have been big developments especially in the material and colour of the boots. But as the champions prefer to stick with the traditional leather boots, this has not set a trend.

Skates can be hired at rinks. In my opinion you should only do this for your first few outings, because:

➤ Every foot has a unique shape. A skate that is constantly worn by different feet will never fit you properly. It is also difficult to get the same pair twice in a row!

➤ It is true that hired skates are sharpened occasionally, but as they are rented out several times a day without a skate guard, the blades soon become blunt and have poor contact with the ice. Also, skates lent to you by friends or relatives should be in faultess condition and fit you well. If there is little progress in your skating ability, this could be due (apart from a lack of interest in skating) not to your own lack of talent, but rather to poor equipment.

So, as soon as you have decided to skate more often, you should buy your own equipment. This includes an all-in-one, a combination of boot and blade. Do not choose the cheapest! These tend to be made of soft metal, which can wear out quickly and must therefore be sharpened frequently; and shoes made of soft leather that give little support to the feet. This is a purchase to last a lifetime! At least for adults, whose feet have stopped growing. Some in-line skates can even be used on the ice: in some expensive models, you can replace the rollers with ice-skating blades.

The kind of skate you start with depends on your interest or your future ambition. Speed-skating shoes are not appropriate. Traditional figure-skating boots are available in white for women and black for men. In contrast to ice hockey skates, they have a heel, the boots come higher up the leg and the blades are less curved. At the front tip, there are toe-picks that are mainly used for take-off and landing when jumping. For the beginner these can be an impediment: they are easily tripped over and will lead to an incorrect push-off from the toe-pick. Ice hockey skates are better value than figure-skating skates: for the same price you can get a reasonable ice hockey all-in-one.

When you buy you should be careful that the boot fits the heel and ankle comfortably. The heel must fit well into the boot, there should only be a little room around the toes. Buy your skates half a size to a size smaller than your normal street shoes. If the boot is too large, then you cannot transfer the movement of your feet onto the ice. You vill "swim" in your boots, have no support and you will easily sprain your ankles when skating and thus feel unsafe. With a more simple boot made of soft leather, you can see immediately if it is too big: it vill wrinkle at the ankle.

Modern all-in-one plastic boots give optimum lateral support to the ankle. However the stiffness of the material means that the fit is not so good as in a leather boot with laces. For beginners and for amateur skaters, however, they can be recommended. They are particularly good for children, as the easily manageable clips provide a solution to the problem of putting the boots on and doing them up.

The second component of the skate, the blade, runs down the centre of the bottom of the boot. However, it is not always the case that this has been set in the middle between the seams. When you buy, test whether you can stand up the all-in-one with the laces done up, without it falling over. This should at least be possible with the skate guards on. You can see differences in quality: you can recognise inferior quality metal by its lustreless, dull appearance. Good quality metal shines. You can see your reflection in it!

Unfortunately, nowadays you cannot go straight onto the ice after your purchase. Your skates must first of all be sharpened. This is usually done by sports shops, or by knife-sharpeners or sharpeners at skating-rinks. If you have figure-skating ambitions, you should point out that the lowest toe-pick of your blade should not be sharpened. This is actually a hindrance for ice-dancing, it's better to get rid of it.

2.3 How Do I Look after my Boots and Blades?

Leather boots should be cared for like normal leather shoes, ie polished occasionally with a good shoe cream. In order to protect the blades from being damaged by hard floors and dirt – it is only possible to skate well in skates with sharp blades – put skate guards on the blades as you make your way onto the rink. These exist also in bright colours nowadays. Take off the skate guards before starting to skate, otherwise your first step on the ice will also be your first fall! After skating, dry the blades with a small cloth or paper tissue so that they don't rust. Don't put skate guards on skates that are still wet. Keep them separate until dry.

2.4 How Do I Do up my Skates Correctly?

Lace them loosely around the toes; tightly from the middle of the foot to the ankle and leave the laces loose in the last two or three hooks. This prevents your toes from being squashed, keeps them warm, gives good ankle support, and allows forward mobility. The same principle also applies for buckled boots. Due to the stiffness of the material, the fit may not be as good as in laced leather boots.

3 ICE-SKATING ETIQUETTE

Don't forget to remove your skate guards before going onto the ice! If you do this once, you can be sure you won't do it again!

3.1 Skating Rules on Public Rinks

On every rink there are skating rules that regulate behaviour on the ice and which serve to protect the safety of all skaters. Basically, everyone should behave on the ice so that they do not endanger themselves or other people.

You should only go onto the ice wearing ice-skates. Normal shoes make the ice dirty, thus creating obstacles for skates and causing unexpected accidents. Dirt can also damage the blades.

Dropping litter and sweet papers onto the ice has the same effect as dirt: they can be tripped and fallen over!

At the rink during public sessions, all skaters must go in the same direction (the same direction as dancing, i.e. usually anti-clockwise). On some rinks, the direction alternates every so often.

Because of the danger to other skaters (skate blades sticking out), no-one should sit at the side of the rink.

On the ice smoking is forbidden.

Games of tag, speed-skating or chain-skating are banned during public sessions.

Apparatus that could endanger other skaters, e.g. ice hockey sticks, etc. must not be brought onto the rink.

Nevertheless, in the following chapters, I suggest exercises and games that require various small pieces of equipment. The actual regulations always depend on which equipment you use, how busy the rink is and exactly how the rink manager enforces the rules in these circumstances. If you use the apparatus so that you do not disturb or endanger other skaters, the rink manager will be more likely to turn a blind eye.

3.2 Skating on Natural Ice

Skating in the open countryside on ponds or lakes is a special experience, You can feel the sun and the crystal-clear winter air on your skin and you can have a wonderful time with all your family walking, cycling, ice-skating, playing ice hockey, pulling the baby behind you on a sledge... and you can bring as much equipment onto the ice as you want!

However, make sure that ice-skating is allowed on the ice by the local authority or the owner. Usually it is not thick enough to be skated on by several people until after a long period of frost, when it measures about 8cm deep. You can recognise weakening ice by its darkish colour, the fact that you can start to see water under the surface, and that its shape changes when you step on it. If there are fissures in the ice or audible cracking sounds, you should under no circumstances venture any further onto the ice!

3.3 What to Do in Case of Falls and Accidents

On the ice, other skaters may often cross your path. When this happens, a collision may sometimes only be avoided if you hold onto each other and so to say hug each other. This way you have more strength to remain on your feet.

Falls can be very painful, especially at slow speeds. On the other hand, at high speeds, they can be relatively harmless, you just glide across the ice. I even advise children and young people to practise falling. Then they are not afraid of it. It's even fun to let yourself glide across the ice on your bottom, stomach or back, or even on your knees, like a footballer after scoring a goal.

Of course, adults are not so keen to try this. If you do fall though, you must try to bring your body under control as soon as possible: fall in a relaxed way and try as hard as possible to *glide* on the ice. The most painful falls are the ones at slow speeds when your entire bodyweight falls vertically.

Break a fall forwards with your hands, relax your arms and let yourself slide onto your stomach. Don't worry about your head, the tonic neck reflex will automatically keep it up! Do protect your head when you fall backwards though (from concussion!), by quickly bringing your chin onto your chest. This rounds your back, so that you roll softly backwards.

Never stay on the ground after the fall, but bring your hands and legs towards your body and stand up as quickly as possible. Skaters coming behind you could find it difficult to avoid you in time.

Figure 4: Falling can be learnt....

3.4 First Aid for Injuries, Blisters and Rubbing

Even the prudent, who know their ice-skating limits, may fall once or twice, but they will not really hurt themselves. If something does happen, it is usually one of the following injuries:

- *Bruises*; these are especially painful after falls on the knees or elbows.
- ➤ First aid: apply ice (there is plenty available!). Scrape a little pile of snow off the surface of the ice with your skate, make it into a snowball and apply it to the injured part of the body.

- *Concussion*; this can be recognised by headache, dizziness, nausea, possible brief loss of consciousness. This is the consequence of an unexpected fall backwards or a collision with another skater.
- ➤ First Aid: Absolute rest, lay the injured skater away from the ice. Call for help (ambulance).

- *Cuts*; They are rare if you wear correctly fitting clothes.
- ➤ First Aid: Cover and keep the wound sterile. Stop any bleeding with a tourniquet. Bandaging material should be available from the rink manager. He will also help you to dress the wound.

More frequent than these problems are those caused by ill-fitting shoes. Your feet can often hurt after just a short time skating. This happens especially with hired skates. The only solution is to rest frequently and then to buy your own skates.

New or hired skates can often cause pressure points or even blisters. If you wish to continue skating, a piece of thick foam can help. Make a hole in the middle of it and put it over the painful spot. Make sure that the hole lies over the affected part.

4 FEATURES OF THE EQUIPMENT AND THE SPORT

4.1 Features of the Ice-skates

The surface on which you stand is called the *blade*. It is curved concavely by a more or less deep hollow-grinding and has an *inside* and an *outside edge*. You skate in a straight line on the width of the blade, you turn by skating on one of the edges.

right edge   blade   left edge

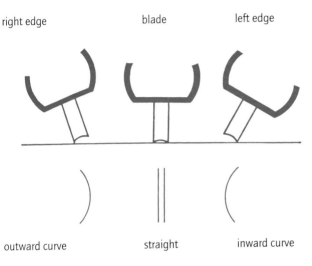

outward curve   straight   inward curve

Figure 5: Left skate in different positions: right edge, blade, left edge and the corresponding tracks left on the ice (see HOFER, page 8)

At the tip of the *figure-skating* blade, there are several toe-picks that are important for take-off and landing when jumping. The blade as a whole is curved convexly, so that there is always only a small part of the blade or edge touching the surface of the ice.

The ideal standing position, the so-called *skating position*, is an upright stance on the middle of the blade, for skating forwards the middle to rear of the blade, for skating backwards the middle to the front of the blade. The weight is on the front part of the skate during turns from forwards to backwards, during spins as well as during take-offs and landings; on the the rear part during turns from backwards to forwards.

Figure 6: Weight distribution during a turn from skating backwards to forwards

4.2 Which Movements Can I Perform on Skates?

Placed at a right angle, the skate creates *resistance*, i.e. you can brake or push-off from the ice. You can feel this by scraping your skate sideways away from the body and then back again towards the skating leg.

A skate can only *glide* in the direction of its *length*. You can experience this when you make "gliding steps": standing with both feet together and supported by the rink barrier, simultaneously push one foot forwards, and the other one backwards, your bodyweight should fall between both legs.

You can stop by standing *on the toe-pick* of the blades: Stand on them while you stretch your feet like a gymnast. Take small steps on the spot; forwards, sideways, backwards, or turn around like a dancing bear.

The blade is hard and rigid. This also makes the sole of the attached boot rigid, which means that on the ice you cannot take long strides as in normal walking, rolling heel to toe. Place your foot flat on the ice in the V-position, almost without gaining any distance. Your toes point diagonally outwards and you glide them actively forwards. Keep your ankles rigid, you mustn't bend them!

Keep your skating leg more or less bent, never rigidly straight. In this way you can compensate more easily for slight unevenness in the surface of the ice and problems of balance. Shifting your weight from one foot to the other is sufficient to let the skate glide forwards a little. The pressure on the ice, and the warming due to friction form a film of water on which the skate can glide. In figure-skating, ice-dancing and ice hockey, the transfer of bodyweight is accompanied by repetitive, rhythmic up and down movements.

4.3 Features of the Sport, or Why it Is so Difficult to Become a Good Ice-skater

Ice-skating requires a very good *sense of balance*. This is due firstly to the very small surface area of the blade, and secondly to the fact that when you skate you are almost always *just on one leg*, and even just on *one edge of the blade*. That is why ice-skating is almost always a *curving movement*, it is rare to move in a straight line on the blade. In addition, your body is inclined, leaning over as you skate along in curves.

Beginners find this particularly difficult. We live in a world where everything is built in straight lines, vertically and horizontally: houses, walls, ceilings, telegraph poles... In ice-skating, this world suddenly becomes inclined! The beginner has the impression either that he or his environment has been destabilised. It seems rather strange, so he tries to stand up straight in order to make everything perpendicular again. He doesn't have the confidence to adopt the sloping body position necessary for good skating on the edge of the blade.

5 FIRST STEPS ON THE ICE –
SKATING FOR SMALL CHILDREN

5.1 At what Age Can Children Start Ice-skating?

As soon as children can walk and run, they can also start to ice-skate. Even 3 year-olds can participate with the correct skates. Only the very youngest should use the so-called "double-bladed skates", skates with two blades on each boot.

Your child can get used to the skates at home, pretending to have a "fashion show". Let him plod around the house wearing his skates (with the skate guards on!). "Stamp the feet loudly on the spot. Turn around, let me watch you from all sides! Continue stamping with small steps forwards, backwards, sideways." In this way your child can get used to the narrow surface of the blade, and learn how to always move the foot as a whole (barely rolling), and also keep the ankle rigid.

Do not demand too much of your child when you venture onto the ice. Do not force him to do anything. Make sure the activities are varied and fun. Set him simple goals to achieve and recognise even small amounts of progress. Leave the ice if your little one is cold or is no longer enjoying skating.

5.2 From Crawling to Standing and Skating

If you want to introduce a small child to ice-skating, a good way is to repeat the process of learning to walk: first crawling then standing. Let him crawl on the ice. Why don't you join him?

Practise standing up from the crawling position: first place one foot, then the other foot under the body. Take the hands off the ice, and straighten the body. You stand in front and reach out your hands for support, if necessary.

Figure 7: From crawling to standing on the ice

Repeat the exercise. The way downwards is already familiar to your child. The hands break the fall, your child then slips forwards gently. So falling and standing up are practised at the same time. This stops him developing a fear of falling.

As a small child must learn to balance on his own two feet, so any new skater – whether a child, a young person or an adult – must learn to balance on his skates. On top of this, he must also get used to the slippery surface of the ice. With this in mind, let your child stamp his feet on the ice, always alternately left and right. Make small side steps with him, to the left, then to the right, then turn on the spot. Try to hold your arms forwards and out to the sides, like a tight-rope walker. Do not help him too much! The aim is to get a sense of balance and the correct standing position on the skate. Your child can only achieve this when he stands up *on his own two feet.*

A clear shift of bodyweight from one leg to the other is essential. You should make sure that your weight rests equally on the whole of the foot. You should not notice stronger pressure on the heel or the ball of your feet. At the start, the foot position is not important. The eventual target, though, is the V-position (toes pointing outwards, heels together) as this is the only position from which you can push- off and then glide.

The foot stamping exercises on skates mentioned probably involved some gliding. This should now be increased: play with your child "Father Christmas in the forest on his reindeer-sledge": "Father Christmas takes four stomping steps forwards. Then he stands on both feet and gets in the sledge. He holds the reins in his hands."

This makes sure that the hands and arms are in front of the body in order to keep the balance. By squatting and bending the knees, more pressure can be exerted on the ice, and the skate can therefore move forwards. The feet should now be placed in the V-position when making the "stamping" steps (to push off), but in a parallel position for the two-footed squatting position (to glide).

If your child is confident and already has experience of in-line skating, these exercises will present no problems for him. If he is nervous, you may need to support him. It is best to skate beside him and support him as in the photos below: hold him from behind with one hand under his upper arm and hold his hand with your other hand. Later it may be sufficient just to hold his hand for psychological support.

Figure 9: The wrong way to support

Figure 8: The right way to support

All other holds are unsuitable: if you support him from behind, then the child will tend to lean backwards, so he isn't balanced (cf. Figure 9). If you skate backwards in front of the child, you can't see where you are going. The child will also tend to support himself on your hands and lean too far forwards.

Figure 10: A gnome as a skating aid

Figure 11: A chair can also be a good support

The rink barrier is not a good support for the child either. It is so high that most children cannot reach the top. Other aids are better, such as stable chairs, traffic cones or specially-made apparatus such as gnomes on skis.

5.2.1 Gliding and Accelerating on Two Feet: the "Egg-shape"

Stand on the ice with your feet in the V-position, your arms forwards and to the sides to keep balance. Bend low at the knees, as if you wanted to sit down. Your feet will glide away from each other, then (to stop yourself doing the splits!) forwards parallel with each other.

his leaves an egg-shaped track on the ice. Make sure that when you sit", your knees and hips are bent with bandy legs. To stand up traight again, pull the legs together again with knock-knees.

Most young children will master the "egg-shape" exercise quickly. It is best to try to perform it backwards too and then several times forwards and backwards without stopping. The aim is to get a feel for the edge of the blade. The inner side of the foot "presses onto the ice", i.e. you can push off from it and thus gain speed.

In the beginning, you will be able to make the "egg-shape" only once, but by squatting deeply and loading the skate correctly (on the middle/back), your momentum will soon increase and you will be able to do it two, three or even more times.

Give your child another goal. Let him skate up to you, or increase the incentive, to make "egg-shapes" around one or more cones.

Now combine stamping the feet (x 4), two-legged gliding and one or more "egg-shapes". Always keep hold of the "reins", i.e. raise the arms slightly forwards and to the side.

Introduce variations, eg through combinations of small arm movements, skating in pairs, or by skating around small obstacles, e.g. gloves, piles of snow, ... : four "Father Christmas steps", 2x squats, two "egg-shape". Skating in synchronised pairs side-by-side or one behind the other. Make the "egg-shape" around cones or other small objects placed a suitable distance (2-3m) apart (Figure 12).

5.2.2 One-legged Skating : "The Stork"

Using the image of a stork, bring your child to his first long glide on one leg: from standing on two legs, lift one leg until the inner ankle is above knee level, the skating leg knee is slightly bent, the arms out to the sides (Figure 13).

First of all practise from a standing position, holding your child by the hands, then without support and without moving. Then carry out these movements while gliding forwards: four "Father Christmas steps"

Figure 12: Doing the "egg-shape"

as a run-up, then short, two-legged glides and finally the "stork". If necessary, give help to begin with by supporting the upper arm and the hand.

Place several tennis balls cut in half or similar small obstacles in a row on the ice. "Move closely past the tennis balls and climb over them with one leg", in other words "stork" left and right alternately.

The stork is easier at higher speeds Combine: a run-up, gliding, one or two "egg-shapes", the "stork".

Figure 13: "The stork"

5.2.3 The First Jump

As soon as your child has developed a good feeling for the correct standing position on his skates, he can attempt the first jump. Put a spell on the lines painted on the ice and pretend they are water ditches (draw these on a pond with thick coloured crayons). Your child should try to cross as many as he likes. He should cross them, maybe even jump over them, on one or two feet. Do not forget to take the spell of the lines afterwards though!

Later, place small, safe obstacles on the ice: a branch, a rolled-up old scarf or something similar.

A pre-requisite for the first *two-legged* jump is that your child should have good balance on his skates. To start with, just make a "hop" without straightening the knees or the hips. In this way there is no danger of leaning too far backwards or falling. Land on both feet with

Figure 14: A one-legged jump

the knees bent, with figure-skating skates *flat on the whole foot*, because of the point. Choose another childish image, hopping like a frog on both legs, or better still: Father Christmas goes in his reindeer sledge down a bumpy forest path. He holds the reins in his hands. At each bump in the ground he jumps out of his seat.

Try this first of all from a standing position: make small bouncing movements. Then Father Christmas goes over a particularly large rock. He goes so high that he takes off a little way from the ground. Finally he lands and sinks back into his seat again.

Figure 15: A two-legged jump

Likewise from a short run-up: four "Father Christmas steps", then two-legged glides in a half-squat position, then jump.

To improve technique, make sure the standing position is balanced, and from which the knees and hips are actively straightened to perform the jump.

Practise the jump in a playful way with different objects: "line jumping" as above, jumping over low obstacles, such as a bar, etc.

➤ Doing a half "egg-shape"

With this technique you can accelerate and also develop a good feeling for the edge of the blades. You perform a half "egg-shape" with each leg in turn. The other moves forward in a straight line, and carries most of the bodyweight. The leg making the shape tries to find resistance with the inner edge of the blade, in order to push off from the ice and accelerate.

This technique is made simpler by using a visual aid: traffic cones, half tennis balls, or similar things. Lay yourself into the curve, just as you would on a bicycle when negotiating an obstacle. The leg furthest from the obstacle carries out the "egg-shape" movement.

➤ Two-legged "slalom"

The two-legged slalom is a technically more evolved version of doing a half "egg-shape". It is different in that now both legs skate in curving lines, and there is a constant change between the inside and the outside edge. Here, the outside edge is used for the first time. You can do this by keeping your legs parallel while your knees bend out to the sides. By pushing off from whichever leg is supporting, you will constantly shift your bodyweight, while you push your feet actively forwards.

With the incentive of a visual aid – skating through a row of cones, or similar objects – you will soon master the basics of the two-legged slalom. To make it easier, take a short run-up, a short, two-legged glide and a slalom through the row of cones, like in a ski race.

5.2.5 Braking

In the "egg-shape" and slalom, you and your child have quickly reached a reasonable speed. That's why it's now time to learn how to brake.

➤ Dodging obstacles

This is easiest when you are skating a curve on two feet, and then let yourself glide to a stop. Children may already consider this to be braking. So that you skate the curve properly, lay yourself into the curve as you would when riding a bicycle: run-up, glide on both feet with your hands leading the way and your head on one side and your body inclined. You are now skating on the edge of the blades and will automatically skate in a curve.

Another way of avoiding an obstacle is to side-step it. To do this, first make preparatory side-steps at a slow speed from a standing position.
    Step over the lines of an ice hockey pitch. Play at bullfighting: hold a towel, your child is a rather skittish bull: he skates towards you and then dodges you at the last minute.

▶ **Two-footed plough stop**
The simplest two-footed braking style corresponds to the technique of the snowplough in skiing. From a two-footed glide, open the legs, and push the heels outwards into the plough position. The skates are thus placed diagonally to the direction of movement and they scrape the ice. Your skates should be flat, and your legs slightly bowed.

First of all make yourself or your child familiar with the *movement possibilities of the skates* (cf. Chapter 4.2): A skate can only glide along its length, therefore only forwards or backwards. If you move it away from the sides of the body it will scrape the ice and produce resistance, i.e. placing your skate diagonally can slow you down and finally stop, or it can also allow you to push off from the ice and accelerate.

When standing on both feet, push the feet alternately backwards and forwards and out to the sides. Your bodyweight should always remain central. Feel how easily your skates glide during the backwards and forwards movements, but how hard it is to move them sideways. Practise the latter with both legs, away from you and back again to the skating leg. This will create small piles of snow which you can use to have a great snowball fight.

Now let both feet glide simultaneously apart and squat slightly: the thighs open and your bodyweight remains central but also shifts backwards a little. It's fun to then jump and return to the closed position.

Now try this braking technique while moving slowly forwards: four stamping steps, a short two-footed glide, sink your hips down and push your heels out. Next try it from a steadily increasing speed, and finally from skating at full speed. Hold the arms forwards and out to the side to maintain balance not as casually as the boy in the photo!

Figure 16: Two-footed plough stop

➤ One-footed snowplough

With this technique, only one heel is brought out to the side and slightly forwards at the same time, i.e. the front part of the *flattened* inside edge of the blade scrapes the ice. So just one skate brakes in the plough position, while the other one continues in a straight line. The main bodyweight lies over the rear leg which is well bent.

Children can learn the correct movement easily with the aid of a small object such as a block of wood, half a tennis ball, a puck, or similar objects. They should try to push the object a little way forwards in front of them with the outside of one foot. Try to play a game

together, each child alternating at braking onto the block of wood.

Try this also with a run-up. Try to stop just before the block of wood, cone, etc.

Figure 17: Stopping with a block of wood

5.3 Enjoyable Games for Young Skaters

5.3.1 Games for Two or More

"The Snake":
The "head" of the snake skates curves along over the ice-rink. Make sure that after pushing off from the ice, the children lift their legs backwards and sideways and not just backwards towards the shins of the child behind them.

Figure 18: The „Snake"

"The Snail"

The same starting position as for the snake, but the children skate a big circle. After a while the first child in the line turns around and skates to the rear, until the shape of a snail is formed, then he tries to find his way forwards to the front again.

"The Caterpillar"

Start as for the snake, but after a few running steps, and having gained a little speed, the group glides on two feet and makes alternately a dwarf and a giant. Each "body part" of the caterpillar copies the movement of the child in front of him. As the up and down movement is out of 'sync' the observer has the impression of a caterpillar creeping slowly across the ice.

"Journey to Italy"

Lead a journey along mountain roads (heavy, stamping steps), with serpentine bends (curve-skating), through low tunnels (ducking), along motorways (fast) and with accidents (falling down), etc. Your child should copy all your movements.

5.3.2 Games with Small Objects

In nearly all public ice-rinks, it is forbidden to bring objects with you onto the ice, especially ice hockey sticks. However, small objects such as towels or cloths, balloons, etc. are not usually a problem. You can place cones at one end of the rink next to the barrier if there are only a few people about. You could even borrow chairs, etc. They are generally tolerated if used for teaching ice-skating. On natural ice surfaces, on the other hand, you can obviously bring anything you want to have fun with onto the ice. Try out all the things you can do with them on the ice. Here are a few suggestions:

Traffic Cones:
*   You can push the cones in front of you with one or both hands.
*   Skate in a circle around a cone. In this way you can have your first taste of skating round in a curve. You can also do this by leaning on it with one hand (cf. Chapter 6.3.2)
*   Place several cones behind each other 1-2m apart. Hide sweets underneath them. Let your child look for them. This is a fun way to improve his stability on his feet.

- The child can skate in different ways around or over the cones: doing "egg-shape", slalom, skating in circles around a cone, then onto the next cone.
- You can enjoy jumping over two cones placed on the ice with their tips together in any way you like.

Chairs
- These can be helpful for the first steps on the ice. They also make skating more fun: if your child is tired or needs a break, he can rest on it while you push it quickly across the ice. It's also possible for the child to push you. As he is not a good skater yet, several children will probably be needed to push you!

Figure 19: A little rest for the coach!

Lines
- *"Line-jumping"*: Draw lines on the ice or use ice hockey pitch markings: these now represent water ditches that can be stepped or jumped over at will. Don't forget to "take the spell off" the lines afterwards! For small children the water ditches really exist!

Bars or Ropes
- A bar lying on the ice or placed or held just above it can be jumped over (cf. Figure 15).

Figure 20: Bar skating together

- Your child can glide under a stretched rope, a bar held at shoulder-height, or under your arm.
- Hold a bar in pairs, and skate while joined together by this rigid axis.
- Likewise, but one behind the other, the rear partner is pulled along. He stands with his weight equally balanced over both feet, knees slightly bent, feet apart and determines the speed by saying how fast he wants to go. An adult can also pull two children using a bar held diagonally or lenghtways.

Figure 21: Games with a bar

- *"The Tamer"*: Stand with your legs wide apart, your heels slightly out to the side (greater stability!) on the ice and hold the bar at one end. Your child grips the other end with both hands and now skates in a circle around you like a horse on a lunging rein.

Balloons and other balls

- Let your child play with balloons just as he likes and let him try out what he can do with them on the ice: e.g. just hold one in his hands while skating, throw one into the air or bat it and catch it again, stuff it under his jacket to make a fat stomach,...

- Ice is a great place to play football. Try it: dribble the ball and kick it around.

Figure 22: Football on the ice

Towels and Cloths

All kinds of towels or cloths are suitable: big and small towles, neckscarves in various materials, shawls, even linen drying-up cloths.

- In pairs, use a towel as a bar: pull your child along behind you, or play at *"The Tamer"* and let your child skate around you.
- Lighter, transparent *chiffon scarves* (neck or juggling scarves) can be put over the face: you now see the world in the colour of the scarf and of course you feel it softly on your skin.
- If you throw one of these cloths into the air, it falls to the ground very slowly. Your child can catch it easily.
  Or try to keep it in the air by blowing.

Figure 23: Towels make good playthings

6 ICE-SKATING FOR CHILDREN AND YOUNG PEOPLE

6.1 Feeling Safe on the Skates

The really obvious, but not always easily achieved ice-skating rule states that: the body or centre of gravity must always be over the support surface (the skate), otherwise – it goes without saying – you will fall over. The correct position, therefore, is where your bodyweight lies over the whole of the sole of your foot.

The best way to appreciate this is by "contrast-learning": stand up straight and bend your knees slightly. Now lean forwards a little so that you feel pressure on the balls of your feet. Then lean slightly backwards, just enough to feel pressure on your heels.

Notice how little you have to move. Now try to find the half-way position: feel how your bodyweight presses on the whole of the sole of your feet, with equal pressure on the balls of your feet and your heels – this is the correct position!

6.2 Basic Techniques

Skating forwards and backwards, skating in a curve, stopping, turning and skating in circles are the basic ice-skating techniques. Only when you have mastered these should you start to specialise in figure-skating, ice hockey or other skating disciplines.

6.2.1 Skating Step Forwards

The skating step, also called "gliding", is the real basic step in all skating disciplines. The footwork is nearly the same, only the body, arm and free leg positions are different.

The main technical points are:
- V-position of the feet, so that you move alternately diagonally to the right, then diagonally to the left.

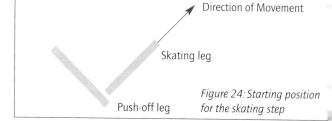

Direction of Movement

Skating leg

Push-off leg

Figure 24: Starting position for the skating step

- The knees are bent and you push off from the inside edge of the blade (not the point!) of the skating leg.
- After a short glide (about a skate length), you may tilt onto the inside edge of the blade, then stand upright gradually by straightening the knees.

► Learning the skating step

You have already prepared this step by practising the stamping step in the V-position. Now make an *active forwards-pushing foot movement*, i.e. bend your knees with each step and push your body forwards over the new skating leg, which now supports your weight and continues the pushing movement.

You can learn and improve the *push from the inside edge of the blade* by pushing away the side barrier of the rink[1]. Place your feet in the V-position in front of the barrier and push off with both hands. Lean forwards and try to "push the barrier away" while making heavy stamping steps, as if you were pushing a car. Then move in the same way on the ice, ideally pushing a partner instead of the barrier of the rink. Finally, try it alone. You will soon be able to go faster.

To begin the skating stop on the outside edge of the blade is the mark of a good speed-skater Lift the inside edge of the foot slightly by turning inwards and put your foot down on the ice. You are now automatically on the outside edge. You can then skate a gentle inwards curve by tilting onto the inside edge of the blade. Figure-skaters, on the other hand, perform the skating step moving straight on on the whole blade of the skate.

---

[1] A tip from my colleague Pocopec, Augsburg

▶ Fun with the skating step

It is fun to practise skating steps through a row of cones:

- Always lean towards the cones after the beginning of the stroke, the skating leg may tilt inwards.

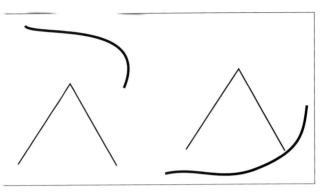

Figure 25: Skating step through a row of cones in the manner of a speed-skater

At least four people are needed for the following games.

"Gliding in Pairs":

- Holding hands, skate in pairs, one pair behind the other. The rear pair accelerates and then glides with their feet together under the hands of the front pair to overtake. Let yourselves carry on gliding afterwards and skate on slowly.
- As above, but all pairs keep together: The last couple glides between all the couples in front of them. Only the gliding couple accelerates, all the others move slowly by transferring the bodyweight forwards, without pushing off.

"Overtaking"

- The same formation and organisation as above, but the last couple let go of their hands and overtake round the respective outside. When the rear pair have overtaken all the people in front of them, they take their place at the front. The next couple starts as soon as they have been overtaken.

6.2.2 Forward Crossover Around the Curve

The forward crossover makes you skate in a circle and for the first time you get the feeling of skating savely on the edge of the blade.

➤ The forward crossover technique

Start off with skating steps from the V-position. When you are moving fast enough, lean your body diagonally (head to the side!) and now place your *feet parallel together* in the direction of movement (a circle!). The leaning position makes you skate on the edge of your blades: the leg on the inside of the circle skates on the *outside edge*, the leg on the outside of the circle skates on the *inside edge*. You should push off from the corresponding edge, not from the toe pick!

Look ahead a third of a circle. Turn your front towards the centre of the circle, so that the outside shoulder, hip and leg are therefore all leading. Place the outside leg inside the circle across and in front of the inside leg, which comes underneath the body next to the outside one. Bring the inside shoulder hard right back. You should be able to feel the resulting tension in your rear shoulder-blade. In figure-skating, your arms show the circle that you will skate. In ice hockey and speed-skating they join in the skating action! In all these disciplines the shoulders are kept still though.

Bring the big toe or inside of the foot of the crossing leg down, in order to skate on the edge of the blades (☞ inside edge). With the inside leg you lift the inside of the foot, so you will move onto the outside edge of the

Figure 26: Forward crossover around the curve

blade. Every time you set your foot down, bend your knees and hips, as if you wanted to sit down. Then glide for a short time on both legs, before you stand up straight again after the next push off. Aim forwards when you push off with your feet by pushing actively off the ice with your foot. Your bodyweight should be central/backwards, never on the balls of your feet, otherwise you will lean too far forwards. The faster you skate, the stronger the lean into the circle and the stronger the forward lean of your upper body.

► One way to learn the forward crossover

Try crossing over first of all with your front to the rink barrier. Support yourself with both hands on it and adopt a leaning position, for example, to the left. Bend your knees as if you wanted to sit down and then step forwards with the right foot across the left leg, then move the left foot so that it is next to the right foot again, and so on. Make these stamping steps and, to start with, pay attention to the inclination of the body and to placing the foot flat down in front of or next to the other foot.

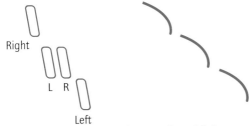

Right

L   R

Left

Figure 27: Foot positions for anti-clockwise forward crossover

Figure 28: Pattern of the forward crossover

Now step over with the right leg bent inwards at the knee. This puts you onto the inside edge of the blade. The big toe side of the foot is low. Place your right foot on the outside edge (small toe side low) next to it.

Then go out onto the ice, ideally in the quieter centre of the rink. Start by standing up straight. Bend your knees slightly and raise your arms to the side. First of all just do a stamping step sideways: in, out, in, out... Position your bodyweight so that you glide forwards a little. Then try to find a middle point around which to skate, e.g. the middle of a bully circle or one of your gloves placed on the ice. Stand about 1-2m away, sideways to it. Look at the object so that the front of your body is turned to the centre. You will feel your body twist slightly. Stamp sideways as before, but side, cross, side, cross, i.e. putting forward and trying to cross your outside foot. If your bodyweight is distributed correctly (at the centre/rearwards), you will "automatically" start to glide. Push your feet forwards actively to accelerate. Adopt a leaning position and try to go onto the edge of the blades. If you skate anticlockwise, you cross your right foot over and stand on the inside edge, then place the left foot on the outside edge next to the right foot.

Practise the forward crossover freely in a circle, eg the centre circle of an ice hockey pitch. If you show the circle with your arms, your shoulders will keep still. Practise as far as possible in both directions. But be careful if you skate in the opposite direction to the other skaters.

➤ Fun Exercises
Practising the crossover with a partner
- Stand facing each other and hold each others' hands. Raise your arms to the side, just below shoulder level like figure skaters. Turn through a right-angle so that the side of your body is facing your partner and start moving with small stamping gliding steps. Gradually lean more towards your partner and start to do the crossover.
- You can let go of the front hand when you feel safer. You should point it in the direction of movement towards your supporting partner though. Try letting go of the rear hand as well.
- As you increase speed, the size of the circle you skate will increase: now pull your partner behind you.

Skate a *figure eight* around two bullycircles at the narrow side of the ice hockey pitch:
- At first, skate on both feet at the cross-over point of the circles. Later try a one-footed transition. It is easier done on the inside leg. Just tilt over from the outside to the inside edge as when stroking. This gives you the correct leaning position for the new circle.

Skate in *snake lines* across the rink (Figure 29)

For the following games several partners are needed.

Crossover in big circles holding hands
(minimum 6 people):

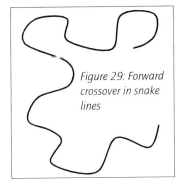

Figure 29: Forward crossover in snake lines

- The whole circle starts skating. Then the "loners" do a forward crossover, the "couples" let themselves be pulled by the others while standing on both feet. After a few circuits, everyone should glide to a halt: Change roles.

The "Tamer" (Groups of three):

- One partner holds two others with his arms stretched out straight; they do the crossover around him.
- This can also be fun as a game of tag: who can catch the others?

The "Wheel" (2-8 people)

- Like the "Tamer", but with an even number of people, i.e. without a central person holding onto the others. ▲-▲-▼-▼.

Figure 30: The "Wheel"

The "Star" (4 – 8 people)

- Hold the left wrist of the person in front of you with your left hand and skate along, doing the crossover, one after the other.
- Likewise with eight people. At each point of the "star", another person is added. The inside person makes stamping steps, the outside persons do the crossover slowly and gently. But be careful, the "outsiders" will speed up due to centrifugal force. Therefore, place less experienced skaters on the inside and more advanced skaters on the outside.

6.2.3 Skating Backwards

You can start to skate backwards as soon as you feel safe skating forwards.

Do not practise this technique to the exclusion of others. Combine it with others that you know and enjoy. With greater general skating confidence, the initial problems you have when skating backwards will sort themselves out.

One problem is that as a beginner, you cannot yet simultaneously skate backwards and look where you are going. So only practise skating backwards when the ice is free enough, or with a partner who skates forwards who can hold your hands and look where you are going.

> **Gliding backwards by pushing off from the side of the rink**

Make your first experiences of gliding backwards with the aid of the rink barrier. Stand facing it, holding onto it with both hands, your legs slightly apart and bent. Now just straighten your arms, to push yourself away from the side. Don't do anything else. Just stay on your feet, and you will glide backwards a little. Let yourself glide to a halt, then skate forwards to the barrier again and try again. Gradually push harder as you straighten your arms, then you will glide back further.

If you feel safe, you can try a game called "pushing your partner". Stand in front of each other holding hands. Your partner skates forwards and pushes you backwards over the ice. Start slowly. Tell your partner when you prefer to go faster. This is even better with a gymnastic bar held horizontally between you.

Figure 31: Gliding backwards by pushing off with the hands

➤ **Increase gliding speed by skating backwards using the "egg-shape" movement**

Stand knock-kneed with your feet in an inverted V-position: your toes together, your heels apart, your weight central, but slightly transferred towards the balls of your feet. Now bend your knees and exercise pressure on the inside of your feet. In this way your feet will start to glide backwards away from each other. Use your muscular strength to pull them together again, thus drawing an egg shape on the ice. Ideally, practise moving forwards and backwards alternately.

Then combine gliding backwards and doing "egg-shapes": push yourself backwards from the side of the rink and try to keep the pace while "egg-shapes" backwards.

You can practise this more easily in the middle of the rink with a partner skating forwards, he can lead you more safely. Don't support yourself on him though. When skating you should always stand on your own two feet.

Figure 32: "Egg-shapes" backwards

Try doing "egg-shape" together. One partner moves forwards, the other backwards. Can you synchronise your skating and adapt to each others' movements?

► Backwards slalom

Stand relaxed, your legs slightly apart and bent. Feel that your weight is evenly balanced over the middle of your skates and over the whole of your feet. Raise your arms to the side and wiggle your bottom as in the "birdie song" that was popular a few years ago. Your feet and arms will turn automatically in the opposite direction.

Can you "wiggle your bottom" so that you move from the spot: forwards, sideways, backwards? It helps if you push your feet a little forwards, sideways or backwards during the hip movement, thus

Figure 33: Gliding backwards

transferring your weight naturally. Bottom to the right – weight to the right,...Don't think about it too much though. Just feel the movement and notice that you load each leg alternately, and can push off from it.

It is even easier when you have built up some initial speed: push off from the side of the rink backwards, glide backwards for a short distance with your feet together and then switch to slaloming backwards.

➤ Backward skating step

In the backward skating step, you skate backwards on one foot for the first time. The technique is similar to skating forwards. But since you are moving backwards, you must adopt the inverted V-position: toes together and heels apart (knock-kneed!). Extend one leg onto the ice in order to push off from the inside edge of the blade. Then raise this foot by simultaneously turning the heel inwards slightly away from the ice. Then place this free leg knock-kneed next to the skating leg again and push off from the other foot. Be careful to stand up straight on the middle of the skate (or more exactly centre-forwards), with your head up. This is a balanced posture.

To learn this step, you can proceed as for skating forwards: stamp along with your whole foot on the spot; transfer your weight distinctly from one foot to the other. Do aerobic steps to lively music: stamping steps ("walking"), maybe with "knees-up", i.e. steps to the right raising the left knee towards the right shoulder and vice-versa. This brings all your body weight onto the skating leg. Then push your weight from the skating leg to the other leg and lower the free foot. The aim is to keep it flat on the ice in front of your skating leg, the tip of your skate low (cf. Tension) and the heel turned inwards. Intensify the push-off and gliding phase.

It is more fun to practise this while holding hands with a partner who skates forwards and looks where you are going. Later, when you have mastered backwards skating, you can try synchronised skating to music. Then try this "pair skating" as a dance. Copy the correct position of ice dancers as you do it.

6.2.4 Turning

Now that you can skate forwards and backwards, you should also learn how to change direction. A pre-requisite for any turn is an upright body posture and good body control, ie all joints (especially the hips and spine) should be fixed and not deviate forwards, backwards or sideways during the turns.

▶ **Turning from skating forwards to skating backwards.**

From a skating step, glide on the right foot forwards and inwards. Drag the left foot at a right angle behind the skating leg. Now start to turn, by turning your head towards your left shoulder. The turn transfers automatically from your shoulder, your hips and also your left foot, whose tip now points backwards. Then transfer your bodyweight backwards and inwards to the left and then put your right foot next to it, onto the outside edge.

Practise this turn while standing sideways to the barrier of the rink, or in pairs. Your partner then takes the part of the barrier, so to speak. With his right hand he holds your left. During the turn, he also takes your other hand.

▶ **Turning from skating backwards to skating forwards**

From a backward skating step, start to glide on the inside edge of the blade, e.g. the right. Turn your head to the left again first of all. This turn transfers "automatically" to your shoulder, hip and then to your left leg. Your left foot should now point to the centre/rear in the new direction of movement. Place it some distance away but heel to heel with the skating leg. It takes the body weight and glides along further on the inside edge of the blade.

Figure 34: Turn from skating backwards to skating forwards.

6.2.5 Braking

You should be able to stop when skating forwards or backwards. It can be done on one or both feet, on the inner or outer edge of the blade. When skating forwards you can:
- stop with both foot
    - on both inside edges = plough
    - on the inside edge of one blade and on the outside edge of the other = hockey stop

- one-footed braking from standing on two feet, i.e. gliding on one foot and braking with the other:
    - at a right angle *behind* the skating leg on the inside or outside edge
    - diagonally *in front* of the skating leg, likewise on the inside or outside edge.

- one-footed braking on the skating leg, with the inside or outside edge (particularly difficult).

Below I explain only the easiest ways to brake (cf. also Chapter 5.2.5, page 38) When practising, make sure you don't brake towards the barrier of the rink or other people. Also allow sufficient room in case of a fall.

➤ Improving braking with the one-footed snowplough
One-footed snowplough braking can best be learnt or improved when skating the forward crossover: as you skate in a circle, you do not need to move the braking leg so far due to centrifugal force. Do a forward crossover, then travel for a while on both feet and turn the heel of the outside foot outwards. The inside edge of your skate now scrapes the ice by the ball of the foot, the other leg skates on as before.

Practise the different "ploughs" with the following *fun exercises:*
- Pull your partner behind you with a gymnastic bar or ice hockey stick. He tries to make life difficult for you by braking from time to time.
- Skate in a group in a circle holding hands (crossing over forwards or chassé): every second person brakes with the outside foot.

Figure 35: Practising braking with a one-legged snowplough

Figure 36: Hockey stop

➤ Hockey stop

Begin this braking technique by rising then sinking. Both skates, or rather heels turn through 90° in the same direction, which means the front skate scrapes along on the inside edge of the blade, the rear skate on the outside edge. The upper body follows the turn so that when you turn the heels to the right in the direction of movement, the right shoulder is also further forward.

In order to learn the hockey stop, brake using a one-footed

snowplough and finally pull the other foot next to it. Try to move the second foot more and more quickly next to the first. Finally start to skate again, making yourself as tall as possible relax upwards and then bend well at the knees, turning both heels at the same time in the same direction.

You can practise braking like this by zig-zag skating: a short run-up, brake, change of direction,... you can lay out pucks, half tennis balls or other safe objects as targets, to skate around at speed and try to brake in time in front of the obstacle. With a lot of fun your braking technique can be improved above all by relay-skating or playing games (ice hockey!)

➤ Braking on the rear of the inside edge behind

Perhaps you already know this braking technique from in-line skating, where it is called a "T-stop". You brake with one foot on the inside edge, so that you place it at a right angle behind the bent skating leg, thus dragging it over the ice.

Most of your bodyweight rests almost all on your slightly bent front leg. The rear foot rests lightly on the inside edge and is dragged almost unloaded over the ice. If you bring too much weight onto it, the edge will dig into the ice so that you will turn inwards towards the skating leg. The same thing happens if the shoulders are not fixed and the opposite arm is not used correctly.

➤ Braking while skating backwards

If you have figure-skating skates, then this kind of braking is really easy. Just lean a bit forward, then the spikes on your skates will stop you. It is a little harder with ice hockey skates. You can brake again with the almost flat skate "behind" the skating leg (seen from the direction of movement it is in front). Try it also on the move: push off with your hands from the side of the rink so that you glide backwards, turn one leg out and place it diagonally, scraping it until you come to a standstill.

A two-legged snowplough is also possible: both legs turn outwards on the inside edge in the inverted V-position.

You will certainly have fun trying the following *games* in pairs:
- Your partner pushes you backwards on the ice. Can you stop him? Or is he stronger than you?
- You can do this holding hands, but it is better to be joined by a fixed axis, e.g. a gymnastic bar or an ice hockey stick.

6.2.6 Skating Curves

As explained in the introductory chapters, the correct ice-skating technique always involves skating on one leg, on one edge of the blade and in a curve. It is very rare to skate in a straight line on the whole of the blade.

Take a look at the track you leave on the ice! If you see two lines close together, then you were skating on the whole blade. If you see just one semi-circular carving, you were skating correctly on the edge of the blade. However, if you left behind a wide, crescent-shaped track you were standing incorrectly on the blade You were not standing on the centre of your skate, and were probably leaning too far backwards. It is also possible that your skates need to be sharpened.

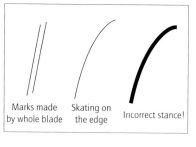

Marks made by whole blade · Skating on the edge · Incorrect stance!

Figure 37: Tracks on the ice

Learning how to skate on the edge of the blade is the most important thing in skating. It is the mark of the advanced skater. It is simplest to skate a curve on two feet; an ice hockey technique, the so-called *Canadian curve or hockey glide:* after a couple of steps run-up, you start gliding forwards on both feet in the skating position. Lean your front leg into the curve, as if you were on a bicycle. Your head leads the way into the curve.

You can learn to skate *curves on one leg* by making longer gliding steps when doing the forward crossover. It is easier to adopt a leaning posture if you skate faster. Make each step last as long as possible. You will certainly find the curve on the inside edge (of the outside leg) easy, as your foot is tilted slightly inwards.

For anatomical reasons, it is harder to skate on the outside edge: the outside of the foot is not as well supported by tendons and ligaments as the inside. You should therefore practise skating on the outside separately. Turn the foot inwards by raising the big toe and notice that the outside of your foot now carries your bodyweight. Skate half-curves through a row of cones, etc. Choose a gap between the cones that allows you to take two skating steps before each one. Then reduce the distance between the cones and carry out your curves directly one after another. Do not skate a slalom though, but nice, round semi-circles!

6.3 Introduction to Speed-skating Techniques

Competitive speed-skating is carried out on a special 400m or 333m track. But an ice hockey pitch is more than enough for learning basic techniques though. Modern short-track (an Olympic event since 1992, track length 111m), is also practised there. For your first experience with this sport you may use your normal skating equipment can be used to get the feel for this sport.

Speed-skating and short-track are cyclical sports, i.e. the same movements, skating and forward crossover steps, are constantly repeated. Skating is always in an anti-clockwise direction. The technical demands are relatively low. But the demands on your fitness are high: speed, endurance and strength are placed in high demand.

6.3.1 Speed-skating and Short-track Techniques

You normally perform a skating step down the straight, and do forward crossover steps around the curves. Good skaters bend their knees very low and lean their upper body forwards until it is almost horizontal. The body's centre of gravity should remain as far as possible at the same height throughout. A strong push-off transfers the weight clearly onto the skating leg with long, gliding steps. The frequency of movements is relatively low.

➤ Skating in a straight line

The technique is largely similar to the skating step described above. The speed requirement entails slight differences in the free leg position and the arm action.

The body is bent like a cat, with a straight back, and the head up in line with the torso.

The push-off takes place from the V-position and after fully straightening e.g. the right leg backwards and to the side. This transfers the body's centre of gravity onto the left leg, which makes a long gliding step. The push-off leg relaxes, the foot hangs loosely in the "slipstream" of the skating leg and swings towards the left. It is then set down under the body and pushes actively diagonally forwards, supported by the push-off from the left leg.

Figure 38: Skating in a straight line

➤ Skating curves

The technique of skating curves is largely similar to the forward crossover technique described above. The skater leaves the straight line by pushing with the right leg into the curve. The extent of the push to match the curve depends on skating speed. The faster the pace (up to 60km/h), the more the skater can lie into the curve.

In speed-skating, the gliding phase during the crossover step is shorter than the glide during the skating step down the straight. In short-track, on the other hand, a regular stride frequency is maintained from the start of the run. Generally, the skater makes three crossover steps around the curve. With increasing speed, he glides for longer into the curve, and makes only two steps, then finally only one forward crossover step, in which he lets himself glide on the inside edge of the blade of the outside leg, in a steep diagonal lean, his hand brushing along the ice. As he comes into the straight, he makes another powerful push-off.

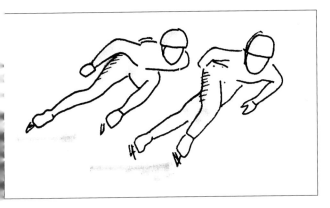

Figure 39: Skating curves

➤ Arm action

The arm action supports the movement. To accelerate, the arms should swing powerfully: the arm should be bent towards the forehead as it swings forwards, and energetically stretched to shoulder-height as it swings backwards, the direction of swing is naturally diagonally backwards.

The arm movement will be drawn out at the turning points due to the length of the strokes, unlike in walking and running "on dry land". Good coordination of skating rhythm and arm action is important. Over long stretches on the straight, the speed-skater holds both hands loosely behind his back. The backs of the hands are towards the body, the right wrist lays in the left hand. Only the outside arm is used when skating a curve. As we always skate in an anti-clockwise direction, this curve is always the right arm.

Figure 40: Arm action

➤ Start

The starting command and technique are the same for speed-skating and short-track: on the command "Go to the start", the skater goes to stand at the starting line.

On "Ready", the starting position is adopted: the rear skate at about 45-60° to the intended direction of movement. The front one is flat or on the forward tip on the ice and slightly diagonal to the direction of movement. The bodyweight rests mainly on the rear leg. The upper body is more upright than when skating.

When you push-off at the start, the front foot makes short, quick strokes on the inside edges of the blade, which with increasing speed become gliding strokes.

The stroke frequency depends on the distance to be skated: it is higher for short distances and lower for long ones. The arm action, coordinated with the stride length, is the same as for athletic running.

Figure 41: Starting position

6.3.2 Learning Speed-skating Techniques

You have now mastered the basic techniques for speed-skating and for short-track. You must just improve them and carry them out accordingly in speed-skating. The arm action described above is not yet important to start with. First just hold your arms so that they are comfortable. The most important thing to start with is that you are well-balanced and that your bodyweight is transferred correctly from one leg to the other. Aim for long, gliding strokes. Try to take as few strokes as possible both down the straight and around the curves.

Speed is not yet important. You can also miss out bending your knees and hips at the beginning. Skate with your body relatively upright, your head in line with your torso, bending comfortably at the knees and the hips. Only bend them more deeply after your fitness is improved by frequent practice and when your skating technique is established.

Practise the skating step down the straight. Just let yourself glide around the curve on both feet to start with. Your bodyweight is then increasingly transferred to the inner leg. The forward crossover should be perfected by practising anti-clockwise: turn your right toe a little inwards when crossing over. The foot should be relaxed, the toes hanging loosely downwards. Push the foot more and more actively forwards onto the ice.

Practise the transition from the straight line to the curve: begin the curve so that when you come out of the skating step, you push off with the right foot as you approach the curve, and transfer your centre of gravity slightly to the left. In the transition from the curve to the straight, try to accelerate by pushing off strongly with your feet, and transferring your centre of gravity back to the middle again.

Use your arms as follows: at slow speeds, skate with your hands behind your back. When you sprint down the straight though, use both arms, but place your left arm behind the back as you start to do the crossover. The right arm continues to swing regularly.

In short-track, tight curves are skated at high speeds. The body leans so hard into the curve that the skater supports himself by touching the ice with the fingers of one hand. Try this with the help of a bollard or cone. Place it beside you on the ice, rest your left hand on it and do a forward crossover. Try to accelerate gradually and to skate in larger circles.

When you can do this almost without supporting yourself on the cones, you are ready to try it on your own.

Figure 42: Using a cone

Figure 43: Perfect curve skating

To begin with, practise the start from a normal standing position with your feet in the V-position, like a standing start in athletics.

Do it slowly at first, then more and more quickly and explosively. Let your body fall forwards and catch your balance by taking several small steps on the inside blade edges.

Then practise the same thing from the correct starting position.

Figure 44: Starting from the V-position

6.4 Introduction to Figure-skating

Figure-skating is all about beautifully executed aesthetic movements and postures. Therefore, skate with a straight back and a proudly raised head, lifting your chest and stretching your neck. Extend your arms to the sides at just under shoulder height, so that you can still see your lower arms and hands. Let the built-up tension spread to the tips of your fingers. Straighten your push-off leg with every stride and keep it extended backwards for a moment. Skate with a swinging rhythm: bend down low at the start of the stroke and then gradually straighten up, while you bring the free leg towards the skating leg.

The basics are described below, they can also be tried with ice hockey skates.

6.4.1 Forwards and Backwards Skating Step

The technique of the forward skating step is like that of speed-skating described above, except for the position of the body and the free leg. For the control of the body it is important to tilt your hips forwards, i.e. the torso is straightened, the pelvis sticks forwards, the bottom sticks out backwards.

After pushing off from the inside edge of the blade, the free leg remains turned outwards and while you glide with extended feet it is kept just above the track of the skate in contact with the ice. The hips are opened and raised, your toes point outwards.

It is best to practise the skating step to music. Skate around to waltz music, for example. Bend your knee each time you stroke and gradually straighten it again, while you tilt onto the inside edge of the blade. Vary rhythm and stroke length according to the style of music.

6.4.2 Forward Crossover

In figure-skating, your arms point in the direction of the circle in which you are skating. So when you skate anti-clockwise the bent right arm is raised to the front, the left points backwards, and the elbows are pulled so far back that you can feel your left shoulder blade touching your spine.

The correct posture of the rear arm can best be learnt together with a partner: do a forward crossover in a circle and pull a partner behind you. He can also do a forward crossover, as in synchronous pair-skating.

Figure 45: Skating in a circle with a partner

You can even do this with three people. The one in the middle will then have both the correct arm and shoulder carriage!

6.4.3 Backward Crossover

This crossover is a technique that figure-skaters use to gain speed before a jump, for example. The technique is largely similar to the forward crossover, but in the opposite direction. Start in an upright position, the front of your body facing the centre of the circle, the side of the body on the outside of the circle, and the corresponding leg are in front. The arms describe the circle. The feet are parallel (not in the V-position) and are placed accordingly. The inside leg glides on the outside blade edge, the outside leg on the inside edge. The push is also carried out from these edges (never from the toe pick). Your bodyweight should be centred well to the front and middle of your skates.

The outside leg is now placed *in front of and across* the other leg. Then the inner leg is placed *next to* it and right into the centre of the circle on the blade or even the inside edge. The foot then glides "radially" outwards, switches to the outside edge of the blade from where it pushes off. The faster the speed, the more your body leans into the centre of the circle.

Figures 46 a-d: Backward crossover

Learn the backward crossover with the help of the rink barrier: stand sideways to the wall, about 1/2m away, ideally with your right side to the barrier. You then skate in the usual direction of movement. Turn towards the barrier and place your hands on it, left to the front and the right to the rear. This gives you the correct body and arm carriage. Turn your body diagonally towards the barrier and do a forward crossover, but push and pull backwards with your hands. Try to stand on your skates in such a way that you glide backwards.

Figure 47:
Using the barrier as an aid

In the centre of the ice, start from the same position: arms raised at the sides, stroke, torso turned slightly to the right. Then make stamping crossover steps to the right, at the same time transfer your bodyweight (central/forward) so that your skates start to glide backwards. Let your feet glide outwards like on a sunbeam. So you will soon master the backward crossover.

➤ Fun exercises to practise the backward crossover

With a partner
- Hold each others' hands, while stretching out your arms to the sides. Turn at right angles to your partner and then start to move around him making stamping or stroking steps backwards. Gradually bend your knees more and more, lean towards your partner and then do the crossover (Figure 48).
- As you feel more secure, hold only one of your partner's hands.
- Then skate in bigger circles. Pull your partner behind you.

"Pair skating"
- One partner does a backward crossover, the other forwards (Figure 49).

Figure 48: Exercise with a partner

"The Tamer"
- As in the forward crossover; one partner holds the hands of two others, with his arms right out to the sides. They skate backwards around him.

"Rotation":
- A big circle holding hands. Only every other skater does the crossover. The others help to start with, then let themselves be pulled along and support those skating.

Figure 49: Pair skating

"Wheel"
- Two, four or, if you are very good, even six people skate in a line backwards. Formation: ▲-▲-▲-▼-▼-▼

"Wheel combination"
- Formation as in the "Wheel" above, except that one person skates forwards, the next backwards, etc.: ▲-▼-▲-▼-▲-▼.

► **Change of Direction**

Using a backward crossover, you can turn towards the centre of the circle (= turn inwards, cf. Chapter 6.2.4), or away from the circle (= turn outwards). If you feel safe on your skates and are confident, you can try both on the ice without further ado. Otherwise, practise using the rink barrier or with a partner, as described earlier: hold hands, arms out to the sides, standing at right-angles to your partner...For the inwards turn, you can change direction again after a few steps without letting your partner's hand go. This is possible because you always turn towards your partner.

For the outwards turn, glide on the *outside edge* of the blade on the leg *nearest* your partner or the barrier. Extend the free leg right back in an arabesque position. Turn your head outwards and backwards and let go with your front hand, your body and leg will follow "automatically". The point of your skate now points backwards, so that you can place your free leg on the outside edge and can skate forwards, away from your partner/the barrier (Figure 50 a-c).

6.4.4 Tips for Learning how to Spin

Spins have a special place in figure-skating. Like jumps and step sequences, they must feature several times in every free programme. There are the following variations according to body position during the turn:
– *upright spins*, i.e. single or two-footed spins standing up straight.
– *camel spins*, i.e. spins turned perpendicularly in a balancing posture, on one leg, with the upper body and free leg held horizontally.
– *sit spins*, i.e. spins carried out in a sitting position on one leg.

These spins can be varied by changing the position of the upper body, of the free foot or the arm carriage. Skaters always find new variations, there are no limits to their fantasies.

Only the two-footed spins in the standing or sitting position should be tackled by the amateur skater. They can be learnt in different ways (see below). Stand up straight on both feet, your body tensed and well-coordinated, your feet slightly apart and turned slightly inwards.

Figures 50 a-c:
Change of direction

Now your skates can make small circles on the spot. Lead into the turn with fast, short bending of the knees and then straightening them. Simultaneously your shoulder turns you backwards around your vertical axis.

As you bring your arms gently towards your body, the turn will become faster. Let yourself just slow down to a two-legged stance and then make a half-turn outwards and skate forwards again.

You can learn the spin by the *"wrapping method"*: imagine that your arms are wrapping paper. Stand up straight (head up, arms out to the side), turn with stamping steps around your own axis.

Your feet are turned slightly inwards, your body is quite firmly tensed. After a few steps, stand still and close your arms in front of your chest, and wrap yourself up.

A simpler introduction to the spin is to skate an inside curve in an upright position, with your right leg to start with away from the skating leg, then pull it energetically back towards the skating leg with the toe pick in front, and extend both legs into the turn.

Wrap yourself up in your arms in order to accelerate the rotation. Open them again when the rotation slows down.

The spin is also easily done following the forwards and inwards circle (cf. Chapter 6.4.6). Do about one turn, then straighten the skating leg and let yourself go on to spin.

Figure 51: Spin

Give the two-legged *sit spin* a try as well. From an upright spin, make a short turn into the deepest squat you can. Do not alter your position on the skates. Then go on to spin on both legs in this squatting position (Sit Spin).

6.4.5 Tips for Learning to Jump

In figure-skating, jumps are always carried out with one or more rotations (up to four!) around the body's vertical axis (with the exception of the straddle jump and the butterfly). There are six rotation jumps: Axel, Toe Loop, Salchow, Rittberger, Flip and Lutz. For all of them, the take-off and landing are one-footed, the latter backwards on the outside edge. These standard jumps are far too difficult for the amateur skater, even with just one turn. But there are easier ways of jumping on the ice, too.

➤ Jumps with two-footed take-off and Landing

You have already learnt the simple forwards extension jump ("frog hop") in one of the first ice-skating lessons. So that the hop becomes a real jump, your knees must straighten explosively and both arms must work in support, as for a jump on dry-land. At first, jump from a low speed, then gradually increase the speed. Land with a "flat foot", so that you do not trip over the toe pick of your skates.

Do the *extension jump* with a *half turn* as well. Land on two feet backwards, hold the landing for a short time on the balls of the feet (= lowest toe pick on figure-skates), then immediately sink onto the whole foot, like jumping on dry-land.

You can learn to jump on your own, but it is more fun with a partner. Stand opposite each other and hold hands. Bend your knees, pull yourselves past each other and make a half-turn, so that you are standing opposite each other again. Then one of you can jump the turn. If you manage this well, both of you jump at the same time. Make sure that you stand up straight before the jump and then jump vertically, as if you were trying to touch the ceiling with your head.

Now you can attempt the jump alone. Support it by using your arms. Choose a speed at which you feel comfortable. The next step is to jump over low, safe obstacles.

➤ Pony Jumps

This jump is similar to the gymnastic jump, the take-off leg is always straight. Figure-skaters like to include this in step sequences.

Correctly done the pony jump is carried out on one leg from the blade edge. For the run-up take one long step with your knee well bent, while your free leg is stretched out at the same time.

Figure 52: Gaining momentum for a two-footed jump

Figure 53: Two-footed jump with a partner

Figure 54: Pony jump

Straighten your skating leg for the take-off and swing the other leg forwards and upwards energetically. Use your arms to support this. During the jump, your body remains upright and tensed, your take-off leg extended towards the ice. You land briefly on the lowest toe pick or tip of the skate of the take-off leg and then, bending your knee well, you set down directly on the full length of the blade of the take-off foot. You should exit on the edge you took off from (outside – outside, or inside – inside).

Now practise supporting yourself on the rink barrier. You can go to the middle of the rink later. Alternatively do it with two partners, each holding your hand and upper arm. Your helpers should be experienced skaters though.

The aim is to skate around a curve into a pony jump, i.e. jump from the edge of the blade. Try it first of all, however, from a forward crossover.

▶ Three Jump

You can imagine the three jump as a step jump with a half-turn. It is always begun with a three turn forwards and outwards, or a Mohawk forwards and inwards (see Chapter 7). You then turn forwards and outwards, bending deep at the knee and skating the forwards outwards take-off curve into the three jump (e.g. left).

Place your jump leg (right) at a tangent away from the take-off curve and straighten your take-off leg energetically. Make a quarter-turn forwards on the ice and take-off from the toe pick. Your legs remain wide apart throughout the jump.

Figure 55: Three jump, shortly before jumping

Figure 56: Three jump landing

The turn is completed as you land on the right toe pick. On the run-out your foot sinks backwards and outwards onto the outside edge of the blade. Your take-off leg is still in front at the moment of landing. Bring it diagonally backwards gently with open hips. Keep your head up, tense your back and adapt an opposite arm position. This stops you from turning too far.

Take note of the fact that the turn is made on the ice, not in the air: a quarter-turn at take-off, another quarter-turn on landing.

You will have fun learning the three jump with the help of a partner. The exercises are still worthwhile even if you practise alone. Carry out the jumps near the rink barrier though, and only go into the centre of the rink when can skate well. Add a half-turn onto the extension jump and repeat the activity in pairs of pulling past each other followed by an extension jump. Try the same with a *one-footed run-up* but a two-footed landing as before, finally also with a *one-footed landing*. Now only one partner jumps, the other supports.

Reduce the help your partner gives you: stand next to each other holding one hand only. Make the three jump as one large, broad step facing your partner, grip the hand furthest from you and glide backwards. Make sure your posture remains upright: head up, don't look at your feet.

To improve your jumping, follow these three tips (derived from HOFER): jump explosively like a high jumper, make your jump leg action like a footballer and the arm action like a boxer.

6.4.6 Games and Fun Exercises for Advanced Skaters

Games increase your competence on the skates and improve your fitness and coordination abilities. They are also a good way to warm up.

➤ Tricks

The "Pistol":
From a squatting position, straighten one leg horizontally along the ice in front of you. To start with, just try "running on the spot" with the aid of your partner:

- Skate in pairs one behind the other holding hands. After a few run-up steps, the front skater adopts a two-legged squat. The partner pushes him across the ice in this position and thus forms the shape of a pistol.

You can also play *"Trains"*

- Both partners go into a squat position one after the other. It is easier for the front one, he can support himself on his partner.

- You can make the *"train"* as long as you want by adding more "carriages" (holding the hips of the person in front).

Figure 57: The pistol shape

The "Fencer"

The technique is similar to a lunge.

- Stand or skate on both feet, then push with a long step forwards into a lunge, upper body and head upright and hips low. The rear foot slides at right angles on the inside of the shoe. Your weight is almost completely loaded onto the bent front leg.
- Skate the "fencer" in cooperation with one or more partners. Try different ways of holding each other so that the exercise is successful and looks good.

Figure 58: The "Fencer"

The "Airplane"

- You probably know the airplane from your school sports lessons: upper body upright, one leg tensed as far as possible in the arabesque position. Try it on the ice:

- If you are very supple, you can grip the blade from inside and pull your leg upwards like an "India rubber".
- You can of course also practise with partners in groups of three. After a few introductory steps, the one in the middle adopts the arabesque position, and then the *"airplane"*. Bear in mind though that, even when you are supported, you must always stand on your own two feet. Feel too that your weight is evenly balanced on the whole of your feet.
- The *"airplane"* is also possible backwards: arabesque in a backwards glide, foot gradually pulled higher.
- See if you can skate an "airplane" with a partner as well.

▲ *Figure 59. Arabesque position*

Figure 60: The "India rubber" ▶

Forwards inwards circle

- This circle with the toe pick dug into the ice looks similar to a lunge with rotation. Stand on the tip of one skate. Bend one knee and push the other leg with a powerful dip of the body in a circle around your skating leg. Pull it forward firmly.

Figure 61: Forwards inwards circle

► Games of Tag

Unfortunately, games of tag are not permitted on public rinks, but there are no such limits on ponds and lakes, etc. In principle, all common games of tag can also be played on the ice, e.g.:

Base Tag

- Do not touch the skater who performs a "gnome", a "stork" or an "airplane" etc., or if he holds onto an object previously designated as a base.
  Make sure that your base is placed so that it does not constitute a danger to other skaters, e.g. clearly in front of an obstacle.

Freeze Tag

- The one who's "it" stands still with his legs apart. He is free to move when another player crawls between his legs. Both cannot be "caught" as this happens.

Criss-cross

- The chaser must always follow the player who crosses his path.

➤ Fun Exercises in twos and threes

Pushing your partner:
- Your partner stands with his knees together and slightly bent. Push him forwards and backwards over the ice.

Pair skating
- Play at pair skating, whereby you copy good figure-skaters with a partner.

Shadow skating
- Go where you want on the ice, a friend follows like your shadow, copying all your movements.

Fartlek (Speed Play)
- Skate along as you wish, changing your speed constantly: from a snailpace to speed-skating, go forwards and then backwards, in straight lines and in curves, you can also add braking manoeuvers.

Human slalom
- You need at least three friends for this. At a distance of about 2m, move all of you forwards slowly. Each respective last person "slaloms" through the human "gates". When he reaches the front, he glides forward and lines himself up again as a "gate".

Overtaking
- Skate slowly in pairs holding hands one behind the other at a distance of about 2m. The rear pair let go their hands and overtake on the outside or the inside, i.e. in the latter case they glide under the "gate" formed by the joined hands of the partner in front.

The Mill
- Stand opposite each other in pairs in a circle with your hands joined and crossed over. One foot is positioned normally, the other at an angle of 90° to the direction of movement. Push off from the latter, and then let it glide heel to heel towards the skating foot. If you attain a good speed, let yourselves glide on with your legs turned out wide, your upper bodies leaning backwards and your arms extended.

Experiment in threes
- Skate next to each other in threes holding hands; the middle skater tries different possibilities of one-legged and blade-edge skating.

Racing
- Try to skate a pre-determined distance as fast as possible with one or more friends.

► Fun with different small apparatus

You can find various suggestions for games with traffic cones, scarves (wool and chiffon scarves), sticks, balls and balloons in Chapter 5.3.2 Try to see what else you can do with these objects by yourself or with one or more partners.

Chiffon scarves
- Three children throw their scarves into the air and catch each others.
- The shoulder and arm carriage during the forward crossover is correct when both scarves float in front of you.

Figure 62: Fun with chiffon scarves – the forward crossover

Cones
- Try out your agility by skating around cones.

Sticks or Hockey Sticks
- You pull your partner along either in a squatting position or sitting on a plastic bag.
- Can you ride on a stick or ice hockey stick like a witch on a broomstick?

Figure 63: Skating cross-legged around cones

6.5 Introduction to Ice Hockey

Ice hockey is a very popular game among sporting young people. More and more girls are also taking it up. There are school leagues and events right up to a World Championships for them.

In ice hockey, you improve your confidence on your skates almost simply by playing. The stick in your hand is a kind of third leg, on which you can support yourself. Unfortunately, it is forbidden to bring sticks onto a public rink during public skating times, and of course playing ice hockey itself is forbidden too. Therefore use natural ice surfaces in periods of heavy frost to play with like-minded friends.

6.5.1 Tips for Equipment and Safety

You have probably seen ice hockey players in action and been amazed at what big strong guys they are: broad shoulders and hips, with a comparatively small head. This does not mean all brawn and no brains. Ice hockey players are in reality normally built sporty young men. They just have to wear bulky protective clothing: chest and shoulder pads, shin pads, etc. The goalkeeper has a strengthened chest protector, wide leg pads that extend far above the knee and a face-shield on the helmet.

Figure 64: Protective ice hockey clothing

You too should wear the appropriate protection when you play ice hockey, i.e. you need at least the following equipment:

Ice hockey skates: on no account use figure-skates. In the heat of combat, it is too easy to trip over the toe pick.

A stick and puck: you can find these in a sporting goods shop. To start with, a stick with a straight blade is sufficient. This will enable you to find out your ideal grip. Backhand passes are easier to make with a straight blade too.

You can determine the correct length of the stick when you stand on your skates: if the stick is vertical to the floor, the end of the stick should reach your chin. Wrap the blade in insulating tape to protect it and give a shock-absorbing effect on handling the puck. If the grip end of the stick is not covered with a rubber cap, similarly wrap tape round it in order to prevent injuries. Never play with a broken or otherwise damaged stick.

Goals: You don't need proper ice hockey goalposts. Any kind of marking which will not cause injury will do. Leave a free space of about 2m behind the goal, so you can run past the goal after attempting to score.

Protective clothing: Always wear *gloves*, if possible with fingers, made of strong material. They protect you when you fall and if you are hit by a stick. You should also wear a *helmet* as a standby. A bicycle helmet will do. If you possess *knee and elbow protectors* from in-line skating or volleyball, they are quite suitable for ice hockey too.

Don't think that these will protect you from all unexpected accidents though. You are not sufficiently protected against a puck flying through the air or against being hit by a stick.

That's why your ice hockey games must look different from those of the pros. The following *rules* should be observed:

Respect each other and play fair. Having fun is more important than winning!

Always keep the head of the stick on the ice. This minimises the risk to players on your team and the opposing team.

The puck should also remain on the ice. You are not sufficiently protected against high and fast shots, even accurate ones.

No intentional jostling, etc!

6.5.2 The Stick as a Skating Aid

You can only play ice hockey well if you can move confidently on your skates and master the basic ice-skating techniques. Using your stick as a third leg will help you enormously to improve your technique. Practise with the ice hockey stick, first without, then with the puck.

Normally, you hold the stick with both hands; when sprinting with only one hand in front of the body on the ice. Use the arms to maintain your balance. Practise forwards and backwards.

You can practise the *forward crossover* most easily on a bully circle or around a traffic cone. Hold the stick at the width of your hips with both hands, the blade of the stick diagonally in front of you on the ice. Lean on it slightly and incline yourself towards the centre of the circle. The stick can be just as helpful when doing a backward crossover.

Figure 65: Forward crossover around a traffic cone

The hockey stop is the most appropriate way of *braking* in ice hockey. Practise it with a stick. It gives you support and forces you to adopt the correct body position: the whole body should stand at a right angle to the direction in which you moved. You should be able to perform the hockey stop in both directions so that you can react appropriately in all situations. Try to start skating again immediately after stopping: toes apart, push off strongly and make quick, short steps. Practise zig-zagging over the ice.

Turning is easiest when carried out as described in Chapter 6.2.4 or by using the "Mohawk" (see Chapter 7.5). Another possibility is as follows: skate forwards and then glide with both feet (for left-handed players, right foot forwards), then make an energetic turn with your hips towards your stick, both skates follow the turn on the ice, and you glide on backwards on both feet (left foot in front). Also practise the turn from backwards to forwards as described in Chapter 6.2.4.

Curve skating: The Canadian curve is explained in Chapter 6.2.6. The ice hockey player skates this in short, sharp curves in situations where he can glide or need not accelerate. Practise on the ice in figure-of-eight patterns around your gloves. Place them wide enough apart (3-4m) so that you can make an accelerated step into the next Canadian curve.

Practise this technique with and without the puck again and again. You will notice how you will feel more and more confident and how your stick and puck control will improve.

▬▬▬▬ 6.5.3 The Stick Grip

Adopt the following *basic position*: legs shoulder-width apart, knees bent, head and upper body upright, stick pointing in the direction of movement on the ice.

Hold the stick with both hands in front of the body: one hand grips the end of the stick, the other lower down; the distance between the hands depends on exactly what you are doing.

When moving the puck the hands are about 30cm apart. When passing and shooting and when receiving passes, the gap should be at least shoulder-width. The lower hand decides on whether the player is called right-handed or left-handed. In the latter case, the blade is bent to the right.

Figure 66: Basic grip

6.5.4 Moving the Puck

You can push, pull or dribble the puck with the stick.

You *push* the puck when you start quickly or when no one is tackling you. Hold the stick with just one hand and turn the wrist slightly inwards, so that you don't lose the puck. Your free arm aids the running action.

You *pull* the puck when skating a curve with the forehand or backhand alongside you or diagonally behind you. Turn your wrist so that you cover the puck with the blade of the stick so it cannot slip away.

Practise pulling sideways, forwards and backwards.

You *dribble* when standing still or when moving, if an opponent tackles. Push the puck to and fro with the middle of the blade in front of your body. As you do so, turn your wrist so that you always cover the puck with the blade of your stick. Practise this *"dribbling"* when standing still at first. Don't look directly at the puck, but keep your head up so that you can see what is happening in the game. Observe the puck only with your peripheral vision. To start with dribble slowly, then speed up, skate in circles, big figure-of-eights, or snaking lines on the ice. Skate in "eights" around your gloves placed on the ice. Try it backwards too.

Figure 67: Moving the puck

6.5.5 Passing

Passing, ie giving and receiving the puck is another basic ice hockey technique. You can only reach a good playing level if you master this successfully.

➤ Giving the puck

If you don't have sufficient protective equipment, you should always pass so that the puck and stick stay low. Practise passes with long and short swings on the forehand and the backhand. To start with, pass from a standing position with a partner. Try to pass onto his stick. Then skate along opposite each other and pass the puck to each other slowly at first, then faster. Change positions so that you can practise both forehand and backhand. The starting position is the straddle

stance, knees slightly bent, your hands about 40cm apart on the stick.
Stand sideways to your target, looking at your partner and his stick.
Look at the puck for just a few seconds before hitting it to make sure

Figure 68: Dribbling (left player)

that it is in the right place on the blade of the stick. Cover the puck as
you make a long backswing, your bodyweight over your rear leg, and
then bring it quickly forwards in front of your body. This pushes the
puck from the corner of the stick to the tip of the blade, thus rotating
it. Level with your front leg, give the puck more momentum by pushing
your lower hand fast in the direction of your target, while pulling the
other hand towards your body (=final snatch). During the pass, your
weight transfers onto the front leg. With a long swing, you can control
the puck well with this pass. It is the pass that enables you to play
most accurately. It requires a lot of space and time though, which you

don't always have in a game. Then you have to play a pass with a short swing, i.e. you swing the stick only a short way backwards, otherwise you can play as described above.

If you are passing to a partner who is moving, you must calculate his speed and that of the puck. Aim a few metres ahead of your partner, to where he will be as the puck arrives.

► Receiving passes

Wait for the puck with your feet wide apart. Hold the blade of your stick level with your front leg. Just before receiving the puck, pull the stick back though, so that ideally puck and stick have the same speed and direction when they meet. Cover the puck with the blade of the stick, so that it can't bounce over it. If you grip the stick more loosely with your lower hand it is easier.

Practise receiving passes on the forehand and the backhand, standing and moving. Try it while skating backwards also.

6.5.6 Shooting at Goal

Every ice hockey player wants to shoot at goal. The action is the same as for the pass. It is true that your target is larger and fixed, but your opponents and the goalkeeper are trying to stop you being successful.

Don't forget the safety rules when shooting at goal: puck and stick remain low. So no high shots and no backswing with the stick in the air.

7 INTRODUCTION TO ICE-DANCING – ICE-SKATING FOR ADULTS

Many adults and elderly people believe that ice-skating is not "in" any more these days, particularly for people of their age. But it is just that their interests have changed: as children and young people they were possibly enthusiastic ice-skaters, then came work, the family and building the house etc...There was no time left for the sport that was one of their favourite winter activities and still is for many young people today.

Older beginners or people taking it up again must also master the correct way to stand on the skates in order to keep their balance and glide forwards. Their first main objective is to skate simple dance steps rhythmically to different kinds of music. First of all, make stamping, then gliding steps, short and long, forwards and sideways (see previous chapters).

When you feel safe doing this, you can learn simple dancing steps and step combinations, as well as skating backwards and braking.

Practise the following dance steps alone to start with. Then try to skate with a partner and to skate together with the same rhythm, direction, speed and stroke length. Ideally, skate next to each other holding one hand to begin with, then skate with a crossed grip in front of the body.

7.1 Chassé

The chassé consists of three steps that are skated on the same curve forwards or backwards. The sequence is 1) left outwards (outside edge), 2) right inwards (inside edge), 3) left outwards (just as right, left right). In 4/4 time, the chassé takes one bar: ♩ ♩ ♩
(Whereby step 3 is held for twice as long as the first two steps, so go left on beat 1, go right on beat 2 and left on 3 and 4.).

Dancing to 3/4 time, the chassé extends over two bars: ♩ ♩ ♩
(Step left on beat 1, 2, step right on 3 of the first bar, the third step is held over the entire second bar.): 1, 2, 3.)

Start from the V-position. During the chassé the feet are however held parallel. The push into the next step, e.g. skating step or chassé onto the other side, is once more made from the V-position.

Figure 69: Chassé

Get into the rhythm first: short, short, long. Stamp on the spot, and then move forwards with small steps. Just rock in time to the music, then the action of rising and sinking to the same rhythm will be successful: to 4/4 time, low (1) – high (2) – low (3) – rising again on (4+).

A technical variation is the *cross chassé*. It is similar to the forward chassé in terms of rhythm and the use of the edges. However, on step (2), do not place the foot next to the skating leg, but cross it over behind it.

The *backward chassé* can best be practised being held by a partner who is skating forward. Later you can do it in the normal dance hold.

7.2 Swing Roll

The swing roll consists of one step only, but it lasts a whole bar, that is three or four beats. It is a dynamically skated curve forwards and outwards. The free leg, turned out and extended, is carried slowly from the back to the front and then it is brought back out next to the skating leg.

For example, in 4/4 time, the sequence is: on beat (1,2) backwards, on (+) it is brought forwards, on (3,4) it is in front, on (+) it is brought back to the skating leg, to be placed next to it in the next bar.

7.3 Progressive Stroking

The progressive stroke has the same rhythm as the chassé in principle, but it consists of only two steps (e.g. left, right) followed by a skating step. It is technically similar to the forward crossover, but the second step is a step forward with well bent knee, so that the feet do not cross over either. It can of course be skated either backwards or forwards.

Using the "foxtrot" movement, combine the following for a simple pattern dance: a stroke left, right, a swing roll left, stroke right, left, swing roll right.

7.4 The Three Turn

The three turn enables you to make changes of direction from forwards to backwards or vice-versa. The name comes from the track that you leave on the ice, which looks like a number three drawn from bottom to top.

7.4.1 Forwards Outwards Three Turn

Start from the V-position, with the skating leg arm (left) in front, the other brought backwards. Skate a gentle curve on the left outside edge. Turn your head, arms and shoulders slowly to the left until the whole of the right side of your body is in front and you can feel the tension in your left shoulder. With a gentle lift from the skating leg knee and an energetic turn of the hips, change from the outside to the inside edge and skate backwards like this briefly. Then set down the free leg on the outside edge and cross over backwards or turn forwards and begin a new three turn.

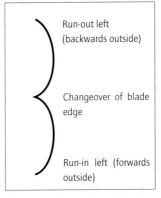

Run-out left (backwards outside)

Changeover of blade edge

Run-in left (forwards outside)

Figure 70: The track made by the three turn

During the three turn you can either close your legs (the feet form a "T") or keep the free leg tensed and extended backwards.

The forwards outwards three turn is a rhythmic step, which is wonderfully suited to waltz music, if you skate just one intermediate step backwards you can turn and skate immediately into the next three turn.

  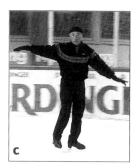

Figures 71 a-c: Forwards outwards three turn

Practise the three turn along the barrier until you can almost manage without holding onto it at all. Don't do too much, above all keep the free leg still behind or next to the skating leg. A dynamic leg action is not necessary and can easily cause you to fall. The edge of your skates are so close to each other so that the hip and shoulder turn is sufficient to allow the change from one edge of the blade to the other. In any case, you may assist the turn with a slight lift up from the knees.

<hr />

7.4.2 Forwards Inwards Three Turn

The forwards inwards three turn is started on the inside edge. The change of edge is thus from inside to outside. Otherwise the technique for the outwards three turn is applied. It is used mainly as an introduction for more difficult elements, e.g. the toe loop and is only rarely skated as an independent step. You will probably find it easier than the outwards three turn; the start and turn are easier as it is begun on the inside edge.

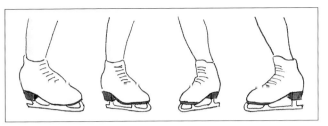

Figure 72: Forwards inwards three turn

7.5 The Mohawk

The Mohawk also enables you to change direction from forwards to backwards. Now the foot changes but the edge remains the same. The *open Mohawk (forwards inwards)* is the easiest, entailing one step with transfer of weight from the inside edge of one leg to the inside edge of the other leg.

Start with the right arm forwards, the left held back. Take one step forwards on the right foot on the inside edge, bring the left heel next to the inside of the skating leg heel (the feet form an "L") and set down the left foot backwards inwards with an energetic turn of the hips to the left. Your shoulders are kept fixed, continue to look in the direction of movement. The right leg – now free – is tensed briefly backwards with the hips open (hence the name of the step) and then set down backwards and outwards next to the skating leg. You are doing three steps, which you can carry out in time with the music, just as you did with the chassé.

You can also practise the Mohawk by holding onto the rink barrier, leaning slightly towards it.

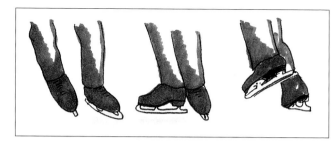

Figure 73: The Mohawk

7.6 Cross-roll

The cross-roll is a step which is skated in small semicircles on the outside edge of your skates. Cross, say, the right leg turned inwards in front of the left leg and then place it on the outside edge. The left leg pushes off from the outside edge and moves you forwards onto the new skating leg. Bend it and hold the free leg backwards and briefly under tension, before you bring it forwards again and place it on the outside edge in front of the skating leg for the next cross-roll.

Figure 74: Cross-roll

7.7 Push Steps

These steps are required for the "Palais Glide" described below. Push your feet to and fro past each other, i.e. forwards and backwards without lifting off the ice. This is accompanied by a rhythmical rising and lowering of the body. During the push, as your legs come together, you should "skate tall". In the final position (one leg is in front, the other under the body), your weight always rests on the rear bent leg (never in the middle). In the "Palais Glide", you transfer your weight on beat (1) onto the right leg, simultaneously pushing your left leg straight forwards on the ice. As you rise, change (2) legs. Now push the stretched-out right leg forwards, pull the left one backwards and transfer your weight onto it, (3) left leg forwards, right backwards, on (4) you stand up by straightening your right knee with a slight lift of the left foot from the ice, and the dance begins again.

7.8 Dance Step Combinations

The dance steps described above, can be combined in many ways. Just let yourself go to the music and skate the steps in any order you like.

Practise them individually at first, then with a partner. Skate *next to each other* holding hands, then nearer together with a cross hold and then the Kilian posture. This enables you both to always skate forwards and make the same steps. Always start with two normal skating steps (left, right), then go into the steps you've agreed to do.

Here are some suggestions for step sequences, e.g. *serpentine step* sequence:
- step left, step right, swing roll left, etc. (keep time : 2-2-4)
- chassé left, swing roll right, etc. (4-4)
- progressive stroke left, right, skating step left, swing roll right, etc. (2-2-4)
- progressive stroke (e.g. left, right), swing roll left, etc. (2-4 = foxtrot movement)
- Mohawk right-left-right, turn to forwards outwards into a left swing roll, chassé right-left-right, swing roll left.

As above, but with a normal step instead of the swing roll and as a *circular step sequence:*
- Mohawk (right, left, right), a half turn left forwards and outwards followed directly with a chassé left.
- Chassé (e.g. left, right), swing roll left, Mohawk (right, left), swing roll left backwards...(2-4).

7.9 Dance and Pair-skating Holds

In all dances the man stands on the left, the woman on the right. The simplest hold suitable for learning the steps is the *front cross hold*. Both partners skate forwards. The nearer arms are crossed forwards and are extended to provide stability and guidance.

In the *Kilian posture*, the dancers also skate forwards next to each other and perform the same steps. The man grips the ball of the woman's left thumb with his left hand (thumbs crossed, palms of the hands together) and pulls his hand towards his upper body. His right hand is placed on the woman's right hip, thus embracing her right thumb. The woman places her right hand flat on the man's. The outside elbows (left for the man, right for the woman) are held out to the side (under tension). It is important again that the woman's left arm and the man's right arm remain extended. This gives stability and only then can the man lead: with the left push to the right, pull to the left.

The *waltz position* corresponds to the normal dance hold on dry-land. One of the partners must always skate backwards, of course!

In the *foxtrot position* the hand and arm positions are like the waltz position. The partners make a 90° turn towards the direction of movement, so that both skate forwards. The joined hands point in the direction of movement.

Figure 75: Waltz position

7.10 Pattern Dances

Learning pattern dances is a special challenge for the amateur skater. Step sequences and use of space are laid down exactly and remain as tracks on the ice.

The relatively simple *Palais Glide* is given as an example. In this dance, both partners skate forwards the whole time. The amateur skater usually finds the cross-chassé and the cross-roll difficult with a partner. Simplify this dance therefore, by skating the chassé instead of a cross-chassé, and a skating step instead of the cross-roll!

Music:
Argentinian Tango or blues, i.e. relatively slow music in 4/4 time.

Dance hold:
Kilian posture

Step sequence:
4 x chassé, 4 x skating step, swing roll left, 3 pushing steps (right, left, right), stretch the skating leg (right).

Key to illustration:

The curved line indicates the path you skate (track). On the left of the pattern the beat for each rhythm is given, e.g. by the start: 1st time is 1 2 3 4 for the 3 steps of the chassés.

The steps to be skated are given on the outside:
L = left, R = right
F = forwards
O = outwards
I = inwards
XCh = Cross-chassé (simplified chassé)
Cr = Cross-roll (simplified: skating step)
SR = Swing roll

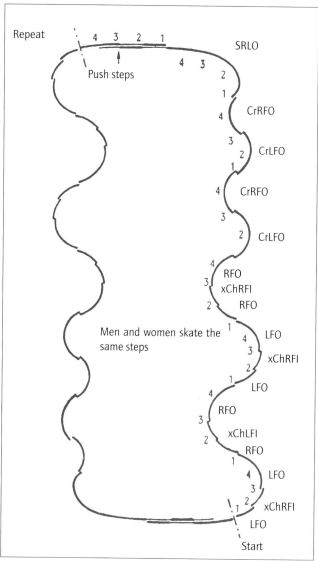

Figure 76: Track for the Palais Glide

EXPLANATION OF THE TECHNICAL TERMS

Arabesque position	With upright body, one leg is extended backwards as far as possible.
Backwards outside curve	Skating in a circular direction backwards on the outside edge.
Balancing ability	A necessary coordinative skill for ice-skating. It enables the body's centre of gravity to balance on a small surface area.
Coordination abilities	The ability to coordinate the central nervous system and muscles while moving.
Curve skating	Skating in a circular track on one leg.
Dance direction	Anticlockwise direction of movement.
Fitness abilities	Strength, speed and endurance are indicators of physical efficiency.
Forwards, backwards, sideways	Indications for direction of movement.
Forwards inwards curve	Skating in a circular direction forwards on the inside edge.
Forwards sideways arm position	The arms are slightly bent (rounded) and held just below shoulder height out to the sides, and slightly forwards. You must still be able to see you hands when you look straight ahead.
Inwards or outwards	Indicates skating on the inside or outside edge.

Opposite arm position	In relation to the skating leg, the opposite arm is in front, the skating leg arm is held to the side or the back.
Opposite dance direction	Clockwise movement.
Orientation awareness	Coordinative ability that gives information on the position of the body in space.
Physical control	Maintenance of a tense posture by fixing the position of the joints.
Reaction ability	Coordinative ability that allows an appropriate response to external stimuli.
V-position of feet	They form a V, ie the heels are together, the toes apart.

PHOTO AND ILLUSTRATION CREDITS

Figure 1:	American greetings card, artist unknown
Figures 4 & 5:	after HOFER, page 8
Drawings:	Lars Banka, Aachen
Coverphoto:	Sportpresse photo Bongarts, Hamburg
All other photos and sketches:	Waltraud Witte
Cover Design:	Birgit Engelen

BIBLIOGRAPHY

ASCHENBRENNER-RATZENHOFER, Herta: Grundlagen zum Lehrstoff-bereich Eislauf. In: REDL, Sepp (ed.): Sport in der Volksschule. Handbuch der Leibeserziehung in der Grundschule. Wien 1909. Pages 218-239.

ASCHENBRENNER-RATZENHOFER, Herta: Eislauf – Skilauf. In: Leibes-übungen – Leibeserziehung 1/1991, Pages 13-16.

BAGUV: Betreten von Eisflächen. In: Der weißblaue pluspunkt 4/1991, Page 4 (Beilage zu pluspunkt 4/1991).

BAUMANN, H.: Handlungskompetenz im Alter – was kann der Sport dazu beitragen? In: OSWALD, W.D./LEHR, U.M.: Altern – Veränderung und Bewältigung. V. Hans Huber, Bern 1990, Pages 52-60.

BAYERISCHER EISSPORT-VERBAND (ed.): Eislaufen. Fortbildung für Lehrerinnen und Lehrer. Kempten 1995[2].

HOFER, Walter: Kunstläufer, Figurenläufer, Freiläufer, Schnelläufer, Eishockeyspieler. Übungsanleitung für Schulsport und Vereins-training. Füssen o.J.

HÜGIN, Otto: Eiskunstlaufen mit Denise Biellmann. Thun 1988[3].

KRAMKOWSKI, Karin: Kinder lernen Eislaufen. Unterrichtsvorschläge zum Erlernen des Eislaufens in der Primarstufe und der Sekundar-stufe I. In: Lehrhilfen für den Sportunterricht, 11/1989, Pages 161-170.

MAIER, Monika: Richtig Eislaufen. München 1979.

MEUSEL, H.: Körperliche Veränderungen im Alternsprozeß und ihre Beeinflussung durch Bewegungsaktivitäten und Sport (2). In: Sportpraxis 2/1995, Pages 7-12 und 3/1995, Pages 9-11.

MORRISSEY, Peter: Lust auf Eiskunstlauf. Stuttgart 1998.

POCOPEC, Josef: Schlittschuhlaufen. Skript für die Studierenden des Sport-Zentrums der Universität Augsburg. Augsburg 1986.

POLEDNIK, Heinz: Sport und Spiel auf dem Eis. Eisschnellauf • Eiskunstlauf • Eishockey • Bandy • Curling • Eisschießen • Eissegeln. Wels 1979.

SCHAFROTH, Jürg (ed.): 1007 Spiele und Übungsformen im Eis-laufen und Eishockey. Schorndorf 1989[2]

SCHNELLDORFER, Manfred: Traumnote 6. Hamburg 1984.

SCHÖNMETZLER, S.: Freuden und Risiken des Eislaufs. In: Sport und Gesundheit 1/1985, Pages 13-16.

WEIDNER, Isolde, et al.: Rahmentrainingskonzeption für Kinder und Jugendliche im Leistungssport. Volume 11: Eisschnellauf. Wiesbaden 1997.

WITTE, W.: Bewegungslehre/Biomechanik des Eislaufs. Skript für die Studierenden des Sport-Zentrums der Universität Erlangen-Nürnberg. Erlangen 1995.

WITTE, W.: Eislaufen in der Schule. Eine methodische Hilfe für den Eislauf-Unterricht mit größeren Gruppen. Skript für die Studierenden des Sport-Zentrums der Universität Erlangen-Nürnberg. Erlangen 1998[4].